REIMAGINING THE KINGDOM

REIMAGINING THE KINGDOM

The Generational Development
of Liberal *Kingdom* Grammar
from Schleiermacher to McLaren

Jeremy Bouma

To Melinda

for your undying support
in more ways than one;
for believing in me
when at times I did not

Reimagining the Kingdom: The Generational Development of Liberal Kingdom Grammar from Schleiermacher to McLaren

Copyright © 2012 by Jeremy Bouma

Published by **THEOKLESIA**
P.O. Box 1180
Grand Rapids, MI 49501
www.theoklesia.com

This title is also available as an ebook.

All rights reserved. No part of this publication may be reproduced, stored in a retrieval system, or transmitted, in any form or by any means, electronic, mechanical, photocopying, recording or otherwise, without prior permission of the author.

Cover Jesus Mosaic image from Petr Kratochvil. Used by permission.

ISBN: 978-0-9854703-9-5

Printed in the United States of America

10 09 08 07 06 05 04 03 02 01

About **THEOKLESIA**

We are a hyperlocal idea curator dedicated to helping the Church of West Michigan rediscover the historic Christian faith for the 21st century. Jesus said that the Church is "the light of the world, a city on a hill that cannot be hidden." We provide the resources to help Her shine brightly in 21st century West Michigan by helping the Church connect God's Story of Rescue to our area, while remaining theologically rooted and biblically uncompromising.

www.theoklesia.com • info@theoklesia.com

CONTENT

Foreword	11
Preface	15
1: Introduction	23
2: Schleiermacher's Grammar	33
3: Ritschl's Grammar	63
4: Rauschenbusch's Grammar	85
5: Tillich's Grammar	113
6: McLaren's Grammar	143
7: Conclusion	169
Afterword	175
Bibliography	179

FOREWORD

I recently received an email from a car dealership that read, "We are incredibly pleased to announce the return of the $14.95 oil and filter change," but only through the end of the month. The email contained a convenient hyperlink to schedule a service appointment and avoid waiting in line.

I happily contacted the dealer, only to learn that the oil change for my car would cost twice as much. I knew this was the normal price for my oil change, so I asked whether the dealer's sale was really a special deal. The service person replied that this was their "new" price (which still sounded a lot like the old one) and that it would still be good after the end of the month. Not surprisingly, I learned that I could not schedule the promised appointment, but would have to cross my fingers and prepare to wait in line.

Wise consumers know to watch out for the bait and switch. Not every sale is actually a sale, and many "free" items end up costing you in the end. Wise Christians must be on guard too. In his classic book, *Christianity and Liberalism*, J. Gresham Machen noted that liberal Christians use terms such as "Jesus," "sin," and "salvation," but they mean something different by them. Machen concluded that "liberalism not only is a different religion from Christianity but belongs in a totally different class of religions."[1]

Jeremy Bouma explains why this is the case in his important guide, *Reimagining the Kingdom*. Liberal Christians from Schleiermacher to McLaren have spoken often of the Kingdom of God. What's not to like? Who wouldn't want the Kingdom to come to earth?

Enter *Reimagining the Kingdom*, a sort of Consumer Reports for Christians. Bouma studies how the liberal giants of the nineteenth and twentieth centuries used the term "Kingdom," and he uncovers a trend that is too consistent to be a coincidence. Just as some sales are not actually on discount, so many who speak of the Kingdom of God do not mean what Jesus meant by it. Specifically, Bouma finds that liberal Christianity offers a different King, a different Kingdom, and a different way of entering the different Kingdom.

Liberal Christianity offers the Kingdom on sale. It's cheaper to enter the liberal kingdom, for new converts do not need to believe such humbling doctrines as total depravity or Christ's penal substitutionary atonement. They do not need to accept that Jesus bore the Father's wrath to save us from

---

[1] J. Gresham Machen, *Christianity and Liberalism* (1923; repr., Grand Rapids: Eerdmans Publishing, 1994), 7.

Foreword

the hell we deserved. It's enough to believe Jesus died to show us how special we are, and hopefully inspire us to follow his loving and trusting example.

The liberal gospel offers salvation at a steep discount, but it's no bargain. *Reimagining the Kingdom* is more than a research project. If you are one who is attracted to the liberal gospel, this consumer's guide might just save your soul.

MICHAEL E. WITTMER. PH.D.
Professor of Systematic and Historical Theology
Grand Rapids Theological Seminary

REIMAGINING THE KINGDOM

PREFACE

Once upon a time I was enamored with the "I-am-not-a-movement-but-a-conversation" known as the Emergent Church. I attended Brian McLaren's church while living in Washington D.C.; Doug Pagitt introduced me to my wife, and later attended our wedding; I helped host the *Church Basement Roadshow* in Grand Rapids, featuring Doug Pagitt, Tony Jones, and Mark Scandrette; I was even known as "Emergent Jeremy" at the seminary I attended. Needless to say, I was deeply embedded in all things Emergent.

My infatuation with the Emergent Church began in late 2004. That year, like many angsty young adults do in their quest to find themselves, for themselves, I entered a period of faith deconstruction and reconstruction the likes of which I had never experienced before. For the first time I was taking my faith in Jesus Christ seriously and asking a whole lot of tough, important questions.

REIMAGINING THE KINGDOM

During this deconstructive, reconstructive season, I stumbled upon a certain "emerging" author, Brian McLaren. I gobbled-up his *A New Kind of Christian* trilogy, because its question-asking, permissive narrative gave flesh to the phantom that was haunting me at the time: What on earth is this whole Christian thing about, anyway? Pastor Dan was my doppelgänger; Neo my mentor. Like many, this series launched me on an entirely new quest to reunderstand and reimagine the Christian faith outside the stuffy, stogy, stale theology that had come to define—and calcify—my evangelical world.

At the beginning, from what I remember when I entered it, the Emergent conversation really was an exploration. Such sites as emergentvillage.org and opensourcetheology.net were catalysts for bursting and burning through the cobwebs and rickety structures of conservative evangelicalism. The Emergent conversation tried to root itself in the more ancient, forgotten parts of our faith—like the Creeds—in order to moor itself while forging ahead with reimagining the Church as centered around the teachings of Jesus and the Kingdom He bore.

Theologically, it was a deconstructive tour de force with its crosshairs aimed squarely at conservative evangelicalism, and rightly so. Reconstructively (is that a word?) it helped construct a missional response to a real, genuine shift occurring within Western culture known as postmodernity. Most of the church was ill equipped to deal with the tectonic shifts our culture was undergoing, and Emergent helped navigate those shifts for church leaders as *New Tribes Missions*

Preface

does for tribal missionaries in Papua New Guinea. At the time I greatly appreciated and benefited from the Emergent conversation, because it intersected with my own faith exploration at the time.

When I entered the conversation around Christmas 2004, I had been ministering on Capitol Hill since Fall 2003 for a little known entity, *The Center for Christian Statesmanship*, of a more well known entity, *Coral Ridge Ministries*, run by an even more known entity, Dr. D. James Kennedy. During this season I became increasingly uncomfortable with the theology behind this thoroughly conservative evangelical ministry, especially their theology of the gospel. The gospel Story it told was rooted in Dr. Kennedy's *Evangelism Explosion*, which started God's Story of Rescue at the end and in the middle—with heaven/hell and sin. Jesus, we were told, came to inaugurate a cosmic transaction between me and Him in order to beam me out of here "some glad morning when this life is o'r."

The theology of this Story disturbed me, so did the methods we used to sell that Story and manner in which we did ministry in our context. You see, the mission context of Capitol Hill is thoroughly postmodern and young adult: at the time there were roughly 24,000 congressional staffers (an average age of 27) who were from the brightest liberal arts institutions this country had to offer. Missionally, we sucked because we were ill-equipped to engage this young adult postmodern culture. Theologically, God's beautiful, majestic Story of Rescue was reduced to five talking points, and Jesus was reduced to a product sold like a vacuum cleaner or set of kitchen knives sans nifty accessories. After a year in ministry I began to wonder: is *this* what I've committed myself too, not only as a minister of the gospel but as a *Christian*?

Then along came the Emergent Church.

My story follows others, me thinks. Many others have endured similar frustrations before wandering into the oasis-village of Emergent, finding solace, healing, and inspiration from a band of sisters and brothers making a similar trek. There, I found what I needed at the time; I am certainly thankful for what Emergent was during those years. I absolutely appreciated the theological deconstruction and missiological reconstruction this conversation provided. At the time, this quest was a healthy and freeing journey that opened up a whole new world to explore and enjoy, particularly the world of the Kingdom of God that I had neither understood nor explored by nature of my own Christian upbringing. For this I am grateful.

In the past 5-6 years, however, it seems like the desire to missionally reconnect the Christian faith to our postmodern, post-Christian culture has faded and the desire to reconstruct Christianity anew in light of both has markedly increased. Now that the Emergent Church has established the missional response to postmodern culture, the time for theological construction has begun. For me, the development of this new era of theological construction is crystalized by four books: Peter Rollins', *How (Not) to Speak of God*;[1] Doug Pagitt's, *A*

---

[1] Peter Rollins, *How (Not) to Speak of God* (Brewster, MA: Paraclete Press, 2006).

Preface

Christianity Worth Believing;[2] Samir Selmanovic's, *It's Really All About God*;[3] and Brian McLaren's, *A New Kind of Christianity*.[4] The Emergent Church movement has indeed exchanged missional engagement for theological reconstruction.[5]

As my relationship with Emergent progressed, I became deeply uncomfortable with this theological reconstructive effort. And as I have progressed in my own academic journey, I have become downright vexed by the theology that has bubbled-up out of the Emergent Church.

I'm not exactly sure when my saucy love affair with the Emergent Church ended. My "I don't" isn't as crystalized as my "I do."

Maybe it was when I read Pelagius' writings and realized much of Emergent theology really does mirror his 5th century theology—and 5th century heresy.

Maybe it was after the former head of Emergent Village, Tony Jones, rejected original sin, claiming that it is "neither biblically, philosophically, nor scientifically tenable."[6]

Maybe it was when I read Fredrick Schleiermacher and realized his and modern liberalism's vapid, gospel-less faith

---

[2] Doug Pagitt, *A Christianity Worth Believing* (San Francisco: Jossey-Bass, 2008).

[3] Samir Selmanovic, *It's Really All About God: Reflections of a Muslim, Atheist, Jewish, Christian* (San Francisco: Jossey-Bass, 2009).

[4] Brian McLaren, *A New Kind of Christianity* (San Francisco: Jossey-Bass, 2010).

[5] You could also lump Rob Bell's *Love Wins* in with this crowd of witnesses, but Bell has disavowed the Emergent label.

[6] Tony Jones, "Original Sin: A Depraved Idea," *BeliefNet*, January 26, 2009, http://blog.beliefnet.com/tonyjones/2009/01/original-sin-a-depraved-idea.html.

are being repackaged and popularized to an unsuspecting, ignorant Christian community as a wholesome alternative to what has been.

Maybe it was after I read Karl Barth and realized the natural theology pushed by popular Emergent theologians is not revitalizing the Christian faith, but killing it; it is the same kind of faith Barth so vociferously fought against in order to preserve historic, orthodox Christianity.

Maybe it was after reading a leading Emergent Church voice suggest that God and grace and the Kingdom of God are not tied directly and exclusively to Jesus Christ; ultimately its not really about Jesus, but about a vanilla, generalized World-Spirit god (lower-case "g").[7]

My growing discomfort and vexation at Emergent theology culminated with a move I thought I would never make: in a widely tweeted and trafficked blog post I wrote two years ago I said "Goodbye" to the Emergent Church.[8]

I had to.

As I progressed in my studies as a pastor and theologian, I came to realize that while Emergent may think it is believing differently—and consequently think it is offering the world a different Christianity that is more believable than the current form—in reality they simply believe *otherly*; the form of Christianity that Emergent pushes is neither innovative nor different: it is a form of Christianity other-than the versions that *currently* exist, but mirror those that have *already* existed.

---

[7] See Samir Selmanovic, *It's Really All About God: Reflections of a Muslim, Atheist, Jewish, Christian* (San Francisco: Jossey-Bass, 2009).

[8] Jeremy Bouma, "Goodbye Emergent: Why I'm Taking the Theology of the Emerging Church to Task," at www.novuslumen.net. February 10, 2010.

Preface

As I wrote back in February 2010, "The Christian faith that the authors, leaders, and followers within Emergent believe 'feels alive, sustainable, and meaningful in *our* day'[9] is really forms of faith from *other* days. They combine other forms of faith that both the Communion of Saints and Spirit of God have deemed foreign to the Holy Scriptures, Rule of Faith, and gospel of Jesus Christ throughout the history of Christ's Bride, the Church." Particularly, the Emergent Church is simply repackaged historic, theological Protestant liberalism for present evangelicalism.

I've shared some of my story here to make it clear that I am not writing as a nitpicky outsider, but as one who was on the inside of and deeply involved with the Emergent Church conversation for over half a decade. Personally, I understand the type of disillusionment and dissatisfaction often engendered by mainstream evangelicalism, while also understanding the pull toward the supposed "new kind of Christianity" offered by Emergent as an antidote. I understand something else, too: the theological problems with such an antidote.

Over the last three years, I have dedicated much of my academic pursuits, through pursuing the Master of Theology in Historical Theology, to better understanding the theological roots of the Emergent Church in order to better understand how it is affecting the Church generally and evangelicalism particularly. That academic pursuit has culminated in this work, my ThM thesis. It explores a trend

---

[9] Doug Pagitt, *A Christianity Worth Believing* (San Francisco: Jossey-Bass, 2008), 2.

within evangelicalism that owes its genesis to the Emergent Church: an increased interest in the Kingdom of God and use of *Kingdom* language to define itself.

Recapturing the Kingdom is a good thing, as it is central to the teachings of Jesus Himself. How some evangelicals are talking about the grammar of the Kingdom—the problem for which the Kingdom solves; the One who bore the Kingdom; and the nature of the Kingdom's solution—is becoming increasingly problematic, however. Though some theologians have noted similarities between the *Kingdom* grammar of Protestant liberalism and Emergent, the significance of these similarities have note been fully explored. Until now.

This book traces the contours of liberal *Kingdom* grammar through four generations of liberalism—from Schleiermacher to Ritschl, Rauschenbusch, and Tillich—that precedes the Emergent Church's appropriation of that grammar for the 21st century American Church, particularly by famed Emergent founder and author Brian McLaren.

I hope this tracing effort will help mainstream evangelicals better understand the contours of Protestant liberal theology in order to better understand how some are reimagining the Kingdom, which is really an effort at reimagining the gospel of Jesus Christ itself.

Jeremy Bouma. Th.M.
Grand Rapids, MI • May 4, 2012
(Commencement Day)

CHAPTER 1
Introduction

In recent years evangelical Christians have rediscovered the biblical emphasis on the Kingdom of God. They have written books, such as *The King Jesus Gospel*,[1] *The Secret Message of Jesus*,[2] and *The Next Christians*,[3] which remind evangelicals that the Kingdom of God lies at the heart of Jesus' mission. They lead mission trips which seek to do more than merely lead sinners to Jesus; they also want to bring the Kingdom of God to earth. In many ways this rediscovery of the Kingdom is right and beneficial, for its advent is the overarching plot line of the Bible. However, as this book will show, its current use often comes with deleterious baggage as

---

[1] Scot McKnight, *The King Jesus Gospel: The Original Good News Revisited* (Grand Rapids: Zondervan, 2011).

[2] Brian McLaren, *The Secret Message of Jesus* (Nashville: W Publishing Group, 2006).

[3] Gabe Lyons, *The Next Christians: The Good News About the End of Christian America* (New York: Doubleday, 2010).

many of its most popular proponents uncritically borrow its grammar from unorthodox historical sources.

The Kingdom of God has not always played such a prominent role in Christian theology, however. Augustine represents the typical manner in which the early church defined the Kingdom of God, equating it with the Church itself. While equating God's Kingdom-rule with the Church largely continued with medieval theological discourse, Christian princes sought to promote an imperial-political view of the Kingdom in order to control their Feudal lands. In the Reformation, Luther individualized the concept for the purpose of emphasizing the Christian's spiritual citizenship over against a citizenship of a secular kingdom. He also represented the Reformation tendency in general to view the Kingdom in entirely eschatological, even apocalyptic, terms that pointed toward heaven in the future. Eventually, the Kingdom played little role in Protestant theology, especially evangelical theology, reflecting the general trajectory of the historic Church that seems to have had little interest in Jesus' central teaching. That is until the nineteenth century.

In the late eighteenth century and early nineteenth century, historical, cultural, and intellectual forces coalesced to foster an environment that gave renewed interest in the Kingdom, giving it a place of theological prominence. The person most credited with such renewal is the German theologian Friedrich Schleiermacher. The Kingdom of God formed the basis of his teachings, governing his system of doctrine and ethics to such an extent that it rose to

Introduction

prominence within theology in a way it had not before. Schleiermacher's voice echoed throughout much of nineteenth century Protestant thought through the likes of Bauer, Herrmann, and Harnack, finding a strong advocate in the theology of Albrecht Ritschl. But while Ritschl praised Schleiermacher for employing the Kingdom of God as the *telos* of Christianity, he believed Schleiermacher did not go far enough in grasping its significance. Ritschl believed Schleiermacher made an important contribution to Christian theology by restoring the Kingdom to a place of importance, but he thought his *Kingdom* grammar was deficient. Building on the original work of Schleiermacher, Ritschl brought this grammar to bear on his entire theological enterprise, making *Kingdom of God* its controlling doctrine. Ritschl's Kingdom-centric theology kindled a new generation of twentieth century liberal theologians, particularly Rauschenbusch and Tillich, who envisioned the Kingdom itself as humanity's salvation.

Now, like the nineteenth century, there has been a resurgence in the use of *Kingdom* language at the start of the twenty-first century, particularly within mainstream evangelicalism. In prior generations, *Kingdom* had not been part of the normal evangelical ecclesial repertoire. Instead, evangelicalism had primarily centered upon the language of *gospel*, which translated into salvation from sins through a conversion experience, personal piety, and moral living. Rarely had *Kingdom* language been employed within evangelicalism. Even when *Kingdom* was utilized, its primary usage was usually future oriented, centering on the return of

Jesus Christ and reign on earth at the expense of its present activity. This definition of *Kingdom*, however, changed with the advent of what has become known as the Emergent Church movement, originally a progressive evangelical movement that sought to re-imagine traditional Christianity in light of postmodernity. In fact, the Kingdom of God is central to the Emergent Church's protest against Traditionalism.

As Jim Belcher explains, "The emerging protest argues that the traditional church has focused too much attention on *how* an individual becomes saved and not enough on how he or she *lives* as a Christian...The critics say the good news is more than forgiveness from sins and a ticket to heaven; it is the appearance of the kingdom of God."[4] This argument, that not enough attention has been paid to Jesus' teaching on the Kingdom of God, has formed the beachhead of protest against Traditionalism, particularly mainstream evangelicalism, and is the central identifying doctrine of this movement. As two prominent Emergent researchers note, the Kingdom of God offers a "reference point for emerging churches" as they deconstruct Traditionalism and reconstruct church in a postmodern context.[5] The Kingdom-way Jesus founded through His life provides a model for emerging churches and actually is their gospel; for them, the Kingdom

---

[4] Jim Belcher, *Deep Church: A Third Way Beyond Emerging and Traditional* (Downers Grove: IVP Books, 2009), 41.

[5] Eddie Gibbs and Ryan K. Bolger. *Emerging Churches: Creating Christian Community in Postmodern Culture* (Grand Rapids: BakerAcademic, 2005), 46. This book provided one of the most exhaustive examinations of the Emerging Church movement. It especially provides an important look at the Emerging Church's *Kingdom* grammar in p. 47-64.

Introduction

saves. No thinker within this movement has sought to redirect the focus of twenty-first century evangelicalism more than Brian McLaren, who helped found the national organization Emergent, is the author of several books that have set out to re-imagine the Christian faith,[6] and was christened as one of the top twenty-five most influential evangelicals in America.[7] He is a fitting contemporary theological dialogue partner, then, in our effort to understand the nature of the *Kingdom* grammar that has surfaced in the twenty-first century, as it did in the nineteenth.

Over the past decade, Emergent generally and McLaren specifically have sought to reclaim what McLaren calls the secret, essential message of Jesus, which he says has been unintentionally misunderstood and intentionally distorted, missed and disregarded.[8] According to McLaren and the rest of the Emergent Church, this message is the Kingdom of God. While many have lauded McLaren's efforts to recapture Jesus' secret Kingdom-message, others argue that his and Emergent's use and description of *Kingdom* is deficient. Belcher writes, "I worry about what is missing in the description [of the Kingdom of God]. It is curious to me that

---

[6] See *A New Kind of Christian* (San Francisco: Jossey-Bass, 2001); *The Story We Find Ourselves In* (San Francisco: Jossey-Bass, 2003); *The Last Word and The Word After That* (San Francisco: Jossey-Bass, 2005); *A Generous Orthodoxy* (Grand Rapids: Zondervan, 2004); *The Secret Message of Jesus* (Nashville: W Publishing Group, 2006); *Everything Must Change* (Nashville: Thomas Nelson, 2006); and *A New Kind of Christianity* (New York: HarperOne, 2010).

[7] "25 Most Influential Evangelicals In America," *Time Magazine*, February 7, 2005.

[8] McLaren, *The Secret Message of Jesus*, 3.

REIMAGINING THE KINGDOM

nowhere does he mention or link the kingdom of God to the doctrines of atonement, justification, union with Christ or our need to be forgiven."[9] Likewise, Scot McKnight believes what McLaren says about the Kingdom is not enough:

> [They] believe that penal substitution theories have not led to a kingdom vision. What I have been pondering and writing about for a decade now is how to construct an 'emerging' gospel that remains faithful to the fulness of the biblical texts about the Atonement, and lands squarely on the word *kingdom*. Girard said something important about the Cross; so does McLaren. But they aren't enough.[10]

The reason contemporary articulations of *Kingdom* by the Emergent Church are not enough is because those articulations are simply appropriations of liberal *Kingdom* grammar.

Rather than offering the Church a new kind of Christianity that somehow recaptures a long-lost concept central to Jesus and the Church, the Emergent Church's use of the Kingdom of God as instantiated in the writings of McLaren is fully entrenched in the Protestant liberal theological tradition, a link several people have already noted. In his book, *Don't Stop Believing*, Michael Wittmer argues that a "postmodern turn toward liberalism is penetrating the evangelical church." He goes on to say that "an increasing number of postmodern Christians are practicing a liberal method: accommodating the gospel to contemporary culture

---

[9] Belcher, *Deep Church*, 118.

[10] Scot McKnight, "McLaren Emerging," *Christianity Today Online*, September 26, 2008, www.christianitytoday.com/ct/2008/september/38.59.html.

Introduction

and expressing greater concern for Christian ethics than its traditional doctrines,"[11] including the Kingdom of God.[12]

In reviewing one of McLaren's latest books, *A New Kind of Christianity*, McKnight notes how this prominent Emergent Church voice "has fallen for an old school of thought," rehashing the ideas of prominent classic Protestant liberals like Adolf Von Harnack and modern ones like Harvey Cox.[13] McKnight has registered such a concern in regards to McLaren's *Kingdom* definition, as well.[14] Furthermore, Belcher voices worry over the Emergent Church's potential pitfall of correlating the Christian faith to culture, which he notes Liberal theology has done for years.[15] Likewise, Belcher worries about what is missing in McLaren's description of the Kingdom, noting that his definition of the Kingdom reduces the gospel and arguing that if his gospel is nothing more than recycled theological liberalism it must be rejected.[16] While these scholars have noted a connection between Protestant liberalism and the Emergent Church, this book will fully explore and demonstrate such a connection.

More precisely, this book will argue that the *Kingdom* grammar of the Emergent Church movement is continuous

---

[11] Michael E. Wittmer, *Don't Stop Believing: Why Living Like Jesus is Not Enough* (Grand Rapids: Zondervan, 2008), 18.

[12] See Wittmer, *Don't Stop Believing*, 110-115.

[13] Scot McKnight, "Review: Brian McLaren's 'A New Kind of Christianity,'" *Christianity Today Online*, February 26, 2010, http://www.christianitytoday.com/ct/2010/march/3.59.html.

[14] McKnight, "McLaren Emerging," www.christianitytoday.com/ct/2008/september/38.59.html.

[15] Belcher, *Deep Church*, 118.

[16] Belcher, *Deep Church*, 116.

with four previous generations of Protestant liberalism, including how it defines the Kingdom of God, who is in, how one gets in, and how it solves for our human problem. In order to understand liberalism's impact on contemporary evangelical *Kingdom* grammar, this examination will trace the generational development of liberal *Kingdom* grammar from Friedrich Schleiermacher to Albrecht Ritschl, Walter Rauschenbusch, and Paul Tillich, concluding that Emergent's *Kingdom* grammar is more or less repackaged liberal grammar. By examining the most prominent Protestant liberals, I will demonstrate a direct link between them and show how they are contributing to the comeback of evangelical *Kingdom* grammar, as evidenced in Emergent's *Kingdom* grammar.

While each of these theologians adds his own unique contribution to liberalism's use of *Kingdom*, there are several features common to this grammar. This grammar teaches that sin is social and environmental, rather than an inherited nature and guilt; Jesus is the moral, rather than metaphysical, Son of God; in founding the Kingdom of God, it was necessary that Jesus lived but the grammar gives no compelling reason that His death was necessary; the Kingdom of God is concerned with humanity's progress; the Kingdom comes into the here-and-now through the power of loving human action; it is inclusive, in that every act counts as Kingdom acts; it is universalistic, in that everyone will be saved; the Kingdom centers on the words, deeds, and suffering of Jesus—His inspiring personality provides humanity the proper example of the universal human ideal;

Introduction

and ultimately, the Kingdom is concerned with bringing the universal human ideal to bear on human existence, empowering individuals and society to reach their fullest human potential and live their best life now.

Understand, however, that in tracing the generational continuity and development of *Kingdom* grammar, this examination does not mean to suggest that each of these theologians is somehow mixed in together to produce one unified *Kingdom* porridge. Not at all. Each theologian provides a unique contribution to liberal *Kingdom* grammar by nature of his historical context and theological development. Yet, they are remarkably similar in their definitions of our human problem, the One who bore that problem's solution, and the nature of that solution itself, the Kingdom of God. In so tracing, we will see how such grammar is impacting contemporary evangelicalism, particularly through its progressive Emergent form.

Roger Olson has said that the story of Christian theology is the story of Christian reflection on the nature of salvation, which is why this examination is important. In it, we will see that the theological reflection offered by progressive evangelicals on the nature of salvation is repetitive and cyclical. While the Emergent Church claims to be helping evangelicalism rediscover authentic Christianity by rediscovering the Kingdom, it is merely repackaging liberalism for a new day. Like liberal *Kingdom* grammar, the Emergent Church ultimately urges people to place their faith in the *way* of Jesus—i.e. the Kingdom of God—rather than the *person* and *work* of Jesus. This is a significant departure from authentic, historic Christianity. Therefore, it is imperative that evangelicals understand the contours of liberal *Kingdom* grammar in order to understand how such grammar is affecting how some evangelicals are reflecting upon the nature of salvation, and consequently how they understand, show, and tell the gospel itself.

CHAPTER 2
Schleiermacher's Grammar

Friedrich Schleiermacher is universally recognized as the father of modern theology. Particularly, Protestant liberalism effectively begins with Schleiermacher as he introduced the theological method and content that would come to define it. Even more pertinent to our cause, it was Schleiermacher who restored the concept of the Kingdom of God to a place of importance after it played little role in Protestant theology.[1] The restoration, and subsequent definition, of that concept would have great bearing upon the development of Protestant theology in an Enlightenment and post-Enlightenment world. As the most influential theologian since John Calvin,[2] Schleiermacher inaugurated a new theological epoch, the

---

[1] Derek R. Nelson, "Schleiermacher and Ritschl on Individual and Social Sin," *Journal of the History of Modern Theology* 16n2 (2009): 144.

[2] Richard R. Niebuhr, *Schleiermacher on Christ and Religion* (New York: Scribner, 1964), 6.

influence of which has lasted for nearly two hundred years. For Schleiermacher the Kingdom of God is the universal realm in which the universal human ideal is active by nature of Jesus' loving example working in and through humanity, which solves for our human problem. Our problem is a conscious absence of relating to the universal human ideal in individual human existence. Thus, we needed a new way of existing, which we find when we follow the influence of Christ's loving example and perpetuate His loving activity. Understanding how Schleiermacher defined the Kingdom and how it solves for our human problem will help us trace this grammar's development through three successive generations of liberal theologians, while also understanding the impact of that grammar today.

SCHLEIERMACHER'S HISTORICAL CONTEXT

Schleiermacher was born into the world of the Enlightenment, the period of European thought and culture that consumed roughly the entire eighteenth century.[3] It was a period known as the "Age of Reason" in which the cultural ethos was defined by a revolt against authoritarianism and gave rise to individual autonomy and reason; the individual rational man was the primary arbiter of truth and action. This reason was not the reason of classical rationalism, but the empirical, experimental reason of Bacon and Locke, which required that the "facts of experience" be examined through

---

[3] Keith W. Clements, *Friedrich Schleiermacher, Pioneer of Modern Theology* (London: Collins, 1987), 8.

the use of a universal, immutable force called Reason.[4] Furthermore, the Enlightenment method led to an ethos of optimistic progress, in which the idealized hope for a this-world transformation became the *telos* (i.e end goal) of modern human living.[5] As Keith W. Clements explains, "the innate and universal endowments of human thought were adjudged to be capable of providing man with whatever knowledge of nature, morality, and religion was necessary for his welfare."[6] Through this seismic epistemological shift, orthodox Christian theology in Europe was pushed toward the periphery of intellectual and social life, because the credibility and necessity for such "supernaturally inspired doctrines" were confronted by "rational, anti-dogmatic modes of thought."[7] This particular contour of the Enlightenment—the exile of orthodox Christianity—(partly) grounds us in understanding Schleiermacher's theology.

Understanding the Enlightenment context only partly grounds us in Schleiermacher's historical context, however, because alongside this historical phenomenon lay another significant movement that impacted his theology and method: the Romantic movement. Romanticism was a reactionary movement within modernity itself that was both akin to and distinguished from the spirit of the

---

[4] James C. Livingston, *Modern Christian Thought: From Enlightenment to Vatican II* (New York: Macmillan Publishing Co., 1971), 4.

[5] Livingston, *Modern Christian Thought*, 7.

[6] Clements, *Friedrich Schleiermacher*, 9.

[7] Clements, *Friedrich Schleiermacher*, 9.

Enlightenment. Rather than a repudiation of the Enlightenment's Age of Reason, the Romantics of the nineteenth century hoped to enlarge the vision of the eighteenth century by cherishing both experience and tradition, emotion and reason, religion and science. As Clements explains, "Romanticism was above all a journey into the inner feelings and passions which constituted the soul and which were to be regarded, ultimately, as a microcosm of the infinite life with which they were in continuity."[8] Thus, contrary to a Cartesian dualism in which Man and Nature are undeniably separate, they are fundamentally akin and variations of the one Infinite Whole; "the sense of Nature's organic unity" is experienced, felt and intuited as an "aesthetic wholeness."[9] Furthermore, they commonly felt that behind Nature a Spirit or Vital Force was at work and immanent in all things, which sharply contrasted with the Deistic "watchmaker God" that was impassively transcendent over creation.[10] It was in this tension between Enlightenment rationality and Romantic passion that Schleiermacher was born, raised, educated, and worked toward recasting the Christian faith for his day. In so working, he pioneered an approach to God that was centrally rooted in universal human experience, as born out of his Romantic context.

In light of modernity, Schleiermacher sought to provide a basis for which the modern man—the so-called "cultured

---

[8] Clements, *Friedrich Schleiermacher*, 12.

[9] Livingston, *Modern Christian Thought*, 82.

[10] Livingston, *Modern Christian Thought*, 82-83.

despisers" of his time—could believe in God. In so doing, he wrested issues of faith out of the hands of both science and morality and placed them in a separate category called "piety"or religious affection.[11] According to Schleiermacher, science concerns knowledge, morality concerns activity, but piety and religion concerns *feeling*. Specifically, religion and piety is described as "the feeling of absolute dependence;"[12] this feeling or experience is the essence of religion[13] and a universal element of life itself.[14] Schleiermacher termed this feeling the *God-consciousness*, which can take on varying forms (i.e. other religions).[15] This feeling is not categorized as *emotion*, however, but instead is a *state of mind*; it is "the immediate consciousness of the universal existence of all finite things, in and through the Infinite, and of all temporal things through the Eternal."[16] In other words, piety and religious affection is the contemplation and self-awareness of our connection with the whole Universe, our relation with God. In fact, he says "to feel oneself absolutely dependent and to be conscious of being in relation with God are one and the

---

[11] Schleiermacher, *On Religion*, 35.

[12] Schleiermacher, *Christian Faith*, 45.

[13] Schleiermacher, *On Religion*, 106.

[14] Schleiermacher, *Christian Faith*, 133.

[15] Schleiermacher, *Christian Faith*, 26, 47. For Schleiermacher, this religious *feeling* plus religious *content* equals so-called *intuition*. Our intuition varies by nature of the varying religious content. Our religious feeling, however, is common among all religions because every person has such a feeling of absolute dependence and connection to God. See *On Religion*, 42-51; 278-280.

[16] Schleiermacher, *On Religion*, 36.

REIMAGINING THE KINGDOM

same thing."[17] Understanding what Schleiermacher means by the idea *God* and its correlating historical context is important to grasping his *Kingdom* grammar.

Schleiermacher describes God as an idea, which "signifies for us simply that which is the co-determinant in this feeling and to which we trace our being in such a state."[18] This 'idea' is the object to which our state of awareness of and connection to something outside ourselves is directed. In a series of meditations, he names this object "the Deity," which is a "poetic symbol of what humanity should be."[19] This is an important definition, as this God-Idea seems to function as a symbol for the highest universal human ideal, which sets the stage for his theological enterprise. Throughout his works, Schleiermacher uses several words that are synonymous for God and this God-Idea: Universe, Deity, Infinite, Eternal, Whole, World-Spirit, and Highest Being. These terms are consistent with the way in which romantic spirituality described God, particularly Neoplatonic romanticism.[20] Schleiermacher's God is conceived in classic romantic spirituality: God is "the Deity," "the eternal and holy Being that lies beyond the world" who is "the Universe that made you," the "One in All and All in One."[21] While some may

---

[17] Schleiermacher, *Christian Faith*, 17.

[18] Schleiermacher, *Christian Faith*, 17.

[19] Friedrich Schleiermacher, *Schleiermacher's Soliloquies: An English Translation of the Monologen with a Critical Introduction and Appendix*. (transl. Horace Leland Friess; Chicago: The Open Court Publishing Company, 1926), 24.

[20] See John W. Cooper, *Panentheism: The Other God of the Philosophers* (Grand Rapids: BakerAcademic, 2006), 80-82.

[21] Schleiermacher, *On Religion*, 1, 2, 7.

insist this language simply reflects his romantic historical context, it is important to realize that Schleiermacher uses these words in place of the historic Christian language of God, because Schleiermacher has replaced the historic definition for God itself with an introspective contemplation of one's "own true being."[22] Schleiermacher envisions grasping this universal human ideal (i.e. God) as my human purpose because it is the very purpose of piety itself: "My only purpose is ever to become more fully what I am,"[23] because God is merely a symbol of what humanity ought be.[24] I know "what I am," the ideal universal human ideal, by finding myself through my "inner life."[25] I grasp "God" not through an external principle (i.e. revelation), but in myself. Hence, religious faith is reformulated as individual human experience. As we will see shortly, this human religious experience through the Kingdom of God is what ultimately solves for our human problem of the absence of the universal human ideal. It is to this problem we now turn.

THE PROBLEM FOR WHICH THE KINGDOM SOLVES

Schleiermacher believed that the Christian faith is "essentially distinguished from other such [monotheistic faiths] by the fact that in it everything is related to the

---

[22] Schleiermacher, *Soliloquies*, 25.
[23] Schleiermacher, *Soliloquies*, 71.
[24] Schleiermacher, *Soliloquies*, 24.
[25] Schleiermacher, *Soliloquies*, 20.

redemption accomplished by Jesus of Nazareth."[26] According to Schleiermacher, the term *redemption* itself is "a passage from a bad condition, which is represented as a state of captivity or constraint, into a better condition."[27] This passage from a bad condition to a better one is directly connected to the context established earlier, for both relate to the theological construct of *God-consciousness*: "We may give to [the evil/bad condition] the name *God-lessness*, or better, *God-forgetfulness*...this condition is nothing but a kind of imprisonment or constraint of the feeling of absolute dependence."[28] *God-forgetfulness* is an "inability to do what our God-consciousness requires us to strive after."[29] Again, in Schleiermacher's words, it is "an obstruction or arrest of the vitality of the higher self-consciousness [i.e. God-consciousness], so that there comes to be little or no union of it with the various determinations of the sensible self-consciousness, and this little or no religious life."[30]

According to Schleiermacher, everyone has the so-called God-consciousness, a feeling of absolute dependence and connection to the universal human ideal (i.e. God). Our problem is we forget that universal human ideal and our life isn't determined by it. Our problem, then, isn't that we have

---

[26] Schleiermacher, *Christian Faith*, 52.

[27] Schleiermacher, *Christian Faith*, 54. Translation "bad condition" altered from "evil condition" by Walter E. Wyman, "Sin and Redemption," in *The Cambridge Companion to Friedrich Schleiermacher* (Ed. Jaqueline Mariña; Cambridge: Cambridge University Press, 2005), 129.

[28] Schleiermacher, *Christian Faith*, 54, 55.

[29] Schleiermacher, *Christian Faith*, 366.

[30] Schleiermacher, *Christian Faith*, 54.

rebelled against God and His ways. Our problem is an inability to "join the thought of God with every thought of any importance that occurs to us;" our human condition is one in which we do not consciously relate to God in everyday existence.[31] As previously argued, the idea of God seems to be taken as the universal human ideal, the image of which is missing from human existence. In his words, "the image of the Infinite in every part of finite nature has gone extinct."[32] We still possess a God-consciousness, but it is missing from our existence. This reinterpretation of sin as the absence of the universal human ideal from actual human experience is further understood through Schleiermacher's understanding of the "flesh" and "spirit," two Pauline concepts Schleiermacher refashioned into a "positive antagonism of the flesh against the spirit."[33] Whereas Paul used the *flesh–spirit* antithesis in eschatological terms to describe the new tension between humanity's relationship to the world versus God in Christ,[34] Schleiermacher defines both in anthropological terms to describe humanity's lower existence vis-a-vis his higher existence.

For Schleiermacher, everything that arrests the free development of the God-consciousness is considered sin, which he explains through his *flesh–spirit* dichotomy. *Flesh* is

---

[31] Friedrich Schleiermacher, "Selected Sermons of Schleiermacher" (Transl. Mark Wilson; London: Hodder and Stoughton, 1890), 38.

[32] Schleiermacher, *Christian Faith*, 241.

[33] Schleiermacher, *Christian Faith*, 271.

[34] For a more complete description of this antithesis to compare against Schleiermacher's, see James D. G. Dunn, *The Theology of Paul the Apostle* (Grand Rapids: Eerdmans Publishing, 1998) 477-482.

conceived as "the totality of the so-called lower powers of the soul,"³⁵ while the *spirit* is a term that refers to man's "inner side, as a self-active being in whom God-consciousness is possible."³⁶ Elsewhere Schleiermacher pits the "sensuous animal life" over against a "higher level" and "higher being," in which man it is humanity's goal to attain the essence of the universal human ideal by turning away from the former in order to grasp the latter.³⁷ It appears that Schleiermacher equates these terms with the *finite* and the *Infinite*, the reality of existence and ideality of human essence. Perhaps Schleiermacher's "spiritualizing" of humanity's goal was a way to counter the earthiness of Enlightenment empiricism that focused on brute facts in order to overcome existence. I quote Schleiermacher at length to explain man's plight:

> Man is born with the religious capacity...If only his sense for the profoundest depth of his own nature is not crushed out, if only all fellowship between himself and the Primal Source is not quite shut off, religion would, after its own fashion, infallibly be developed...*I see how all things unite to bind man to the finite...that the Infinite may as far as possible vanish from their eyes.*³⁸

He further says we have consciousness of sin whenever "the God-Consciousness...determines our self-consciousness as pain," which Wyman rightly interprets as experiencing "a sense of incompleteness, mental discomfort, of things

---

³⁵ Schleiermacher, *Christian Faith*, 271.

³⁶ Schleiermacher, *Christian Faith*, 238.

³⁷ Schleiermacher, *Soliloquies*, 30, 31.

³⁸ Schleiermacher, *On Religion*, 124-125. (emph. mine)

somehow out of joint, of the world lacking religious meaning."[39] In other words, we sense a disconnect between our existence and the universal ideal, between the so-called "sensible-consciousness"[40] (flesh) that conditions his existence and the God-consciousness (spirit) that conditions the essence of humanity. According to Schleiermacher, this disconnection is traced to the beginning of man's development itself.

Unlike the historic Christian faith that roots man's sinful condition in the Augustinian concept of *original sin*, Schleiermacher dismisses the idea of a pre-Fall idyllic state. As he says, "we have no reason for explaining universal sinfulness as due to an alteration in human nature brought about [by the first human pair] by the first sin."[41] He does not want to say human nature in anyway was changed, but instead "human nature was the same before the first sin as it appears subsequently alike in them and their posterity."[42] In fact, he suggests that Adam must have already been apart from God

---

[39] Wyman, "Sin and Redemption," 133.

[40] The *sensible-consciousness* constitutes "the whole field of experience in the widest sense of the word and...all determinations of self-consciousness which develop from our relations to nature and to man." (CF, 19) It is the normal sphere of consciousness that man experiences in relation to his worldly existence. It is a *lower consciousness* set over against the *higher consciousness* man experiences in relation to "God." In the only example Schleiermacher gives in this discussion, he states there can be "a sorrow of the lower and a joy of the higher self-consciousness, as for example whenever with a feeling of suffering there is combined a trust in God." (CF, 24) Thus, existence is given meaning when there is an awareness of and relationship to God, the ideal. The inhibition of this awareness (i.e. God-consciousness) is what constitutes the "bad condition."

[41] Schleiermacher, *Christian Faith*, 291.

[42] Schleiermacher, *Christian Faith*, 296.

before his first sin, leading him to reject the traditional formulation of human nature (i.e. original sin) in favor of a new one: "persons corrupt themselves and one another."[43] He says this is "an adequate description of all the sin that ever appears amongst man" because it keeps nature out of the matter and places the genesis of sin outside ourselves. Instead of placing the shift toward sin in human *nature*, Schleiermacher places the shift toward sin in human *history*: sinfulness operates in individuals "through the sin and sinfulness of others...it is transmitted by the voluntary actions of every individual to others and implanted within them."[44] As he famously said: "in each the work of all, and indeed all the work of each."[45] There is a universal sinfulness, because of a "corporate consciousness" of sin; a solidarity exists in humanity across time and space in which the total existence of those sharing a common life combine to form an "aggregate power of the flesh" that is opposed to the spirit.[46] Individuals exist in families and clans and communities in which the God-consciousness is already deficient and obstructed, manifesting and perpetuating that history in their own existence.

Note the underlying Pelagianism inherent in Schleiermacher's reformulation of the human condition: bad examples from the community form bad habits in the individual, which perpetuate the bad condition discussed

---

[43] Schleiermacher, *Christian Faith*, 298.
[44] Schleiermacher, *Christian Faith*, 287.
[45] Schleiermacher, *Christian Faith*, 288.
[46] Schleiermacher, *Christian Faith*, 288.

Schleiermacher's Grammar

earlier that suppresses the universal human ideal (i.e. God-consciousness) in existence. The result, according to Schleiermacher, is that "throughout the entire range of sinful humanity there is not a single perfectly good action, that is, one that purely expresses the power of the God-consciousness; nor is there one perfectly pure moment, that is, one in which something does not exist in secret antagonism to the God-consciousness."[47] And this leads to our definition of sin itself.

Schleiermacher writes, "what gives a moment the character of sin is the self-centered activity of the flesh...for all activities of the flesh are good when subservient to the spirit and all are evil when severed from it." Here sin is located in human consciousness, as perpetuated by the human community, which results in actual sin—which Fries notes is "the sinful condition and action of the individual giving expression to the sin of the race."[48] These self-centered activities add to the "force of habit and thus the vitiation of the God-consciousness," which "spreads and establishes itself by communication to others."[49] This vitiation, or impairment, of the God-consciousness—our connection to and relationship with the universal human ideal—*is* sin, and this impairment is "inherited" from one person to the next through bad examples and the habit wrought through following those bad examples, resulting in social and moral

---

[47] Schleiermacher, *Christian Faith*, 305.

[48] Paul Roy Fries, "Religion and the Hope for a Truly Human Existence" (PhD diss., Utrecht University, 1979), 61.

[49] Schleiermacher, *Christian Faith*, 313.

evils that fail to realize the universal human ideal. Therefore, the individual is guilty for having participated in the human incapacity for the human ideal and perpetuating faulty human existence, resulting in "a complete incapacity for the good, which can be removed only by the influence of Redemption."[50] Humanity needed a redeemer, then, to do something with that faulty human existence and help us "remember" our God-consciousness, to remember the universal human ideal. We found such a Redeemer in Jesus, who stopped the perpetuation of God-forgetfulness by destroying 'originating' original sin through His loving life example, while completing humanity through that life.

THE BEARER OF THE KINGDOM: THE PERSON AND WORK OF JESUS

According to Schleiermacher, Christianity is the most developed form of religion, because of the person who exhibited the highest human ideal: Jesus of Nazareth.[51] Schleiermacher describes Jesus as having "an absolutely powerful God-consciousness," in Him was a "constant potency of God-consciousness, which was a veritable existence of God in him."[52] In Christ we see God active—which is equated with the existence of God;[53] all His activities proceeded from "the being of God in Him"[54] —

---

[50] Schleiermacher, *Christian Faith*, 282.

[51] Schleiermacher, *Christian Faith*, 38.

[52] Schleiermacher, *Christian Faith*, 387.

[53] Schleiermacher, *Christian Faith*, 387.

[54] Schleiermacher, *Christian Faith*, 426.

which seems to be the universal human ideal working in and through His life. This principle—the being of God—is timeless and eternal, but expressed itself temporally in Jesus' human life.[55] Thus, His life was determined by the universal human ideal that revealed itself in human existence, because He possessed the God-consciousness in its fullness. This doesn't mean Jesus was God Himself. Instead it means Jesus somehow grasped, in word and deed, the highest human spirit. It would help to quote Schleiermacher at length in order to understand how he conceived of Jesus' divinity:

> if it is only through Him that the human God-consciousness became an existence of God in human nature, and only through the rational nature that the totality of the finite powers can become an existence of God in the world, that in truth He alone mediates all existence of God in the world and all revelation of God through the world, in so far as He bears within Himself the whole new creation which contains and develops the potency of the God-consciousness.[56]

Notice that as the "revelation of God" Jesus possessed the new creation, which is the fully potent God-consciousness, the universal human ideal realized in human existence. Consequently, Jesus is considered the completion and perfection of humanity by nature of His potent God-consciousness.

As Schleiermacher plainly puts it, Jesus is "the One in whom the human creation is perfected..." As the Second

---

[55] Schleiermacher, *Christian Faith*, 426.

[56] Schleiermacher, *Christian Faith*, 388.

Adam Jesus is "altogether like all those who are descended from the first, only that from the outset He has an absolutely potent God-consciousness....His whole activity stands under the law of historical development, and that activity is brought to perfection through the gradual expansion, from the point at which He appears, over the whole."[57] Schleiermacher maintained that at the beginning of His life, Jesus had a "new implanting of the God-consciousness," which Schleiermacher regarded as the completed creation of human nature itself. It is this universal human ideal—the being of God and God-consciousness—that Jesus sought to impart to His followers through His earthly life. The imparting of His God-consciousness comes about through a strengthening of that state of awareness and an assumption of the believer into the power of His own God-consciousness.[58] In Schleiermacher's words, Jesus' whole redemptive mission was "to raise men to fellowship with God and to rule spiritually," to grasp the feeling of dependence and relation to the universal human ideal. This was His redeeming activity, accomplished by founding a new fellowship, a new corporate life: the Kingdom of God.

Schleiermacher frames our problem's solution and Jesus' work in terms of a *state of blessedness* that is rooted in the corporate life of the Kingdom. He writes, "We are conscious that all approximations to the state of blessedness which occurs in the Christian life as being grounded in a new divinely-effected corporate life, which works in opposition to

---

[57] Schleiermacher, *Christian Faith*, 367.
[58] Schleiermacher, *Christian Faith*, 425.

the corporate life of sin and the misery which develops in it."[59] This blessedness of Christ signifies none other than the completion, or perfection, of humanity: "the appearance of Christ and the institution of this new corporate life [i.e. Kingdom of God] would have to be regarded as the completion, only now accomplished of the creation of humanity."[60] In the first stage of human existence, humanity was "under the law of earthly existence," existing in the "sensuous animal life" and sensuous self-consciousness, while the "higher life" and God-consciousness only gradually came later; the God-consciousness that began in the first stage was "inadequate and impotent."[61] In this second stage, however, the God-consciousness "broke forth in perfection in Christ, from whom it continually extends its authority, and proves its power to bring peace and blessedness to men,"[62] which is the ever expanding Kingdom of God instantiated in the ever-expanding loving activity of humanity. This human activity is the crux of Jesus' redemptive work; Jesus "redeems" humanity when they follow His loving example and perpetuate His loving activity.

Schleiermacher believed the essence of the work of Jesus is "that the God-consciousness already present in human nature, though feeble and repressed, becomes stimulated and made dominant by the entrance of the living influence of

---

[59] Schleiermacher, *Christian Faith*, 358.

[60] Schleiermacher, *Christian Faith*, 366.

[61] Schleiermacher, *Christian Faith*, 368.

[62] Schleiermacher, *Christian Faith*, 368.

Christ..."⁶³ The redemptive work of Christ is essentially His *living*, rather than his dying. Though Schleiermacher does not deny the importance of the cross, it is important insofar as it is an extension and climax of Jesus' life; the cross is simply the greatest act of love, the greatest in a long series of loving actions that have reverberated throughout history. Redemption takes place, then, when "The Redeemer assumes believers into the power of His God-consciousness, and this is his redemptive activity."⁶⁴ This assumption takes place when the individual takes upon himself the influence of Christ by following His example of love and perpetuates His life of love. As Schleiermacher writes, "the total effective influence of Christ is only the continuation of the creative divine activity out of which the Person of Christ arose. For this, too, was directed towards human nature as a whole, in which that being of God was to exist, but in such a way that its effects are mediated through the life of Christ..."⁶⁵ So the universal human ideal (i.e. being of God) was to exist in human nature as a whole, and the effect of it is mediated to humanity through Christ's life-example and influence, so that "the former personality may be slain and human nature...be formed into persons in totality of that higher life."⁶⁶ In other words, the goal of redemption is that the sensuous-conscious of real human existence might be replaced with the God-consciousness of the ideal human essence, which occurs in the

---

⁶³ Schleiermacher, *Christian Faith*, 476.

⁶⁴ Schleiermacher, *Christian Faith*, 425.

⁶⁵ Schleiermacher, *Christian Faith*, 427.

⁶⁶ Schleiermacher, *Christian Faith*, 428.

corporate life of the Kingdom, the true nature of Jesus' redemptive work.

It is through the corporate life of the Kingdom of God that "fallen" human existence is resolved and humanity itself is redeemed. The redemptive work of Jesus is the life He lived, perpetuated in the Kingdom He founded. This redemption is effected in humanity when the sinless perfection of Jesus is "communicated" to it.[67] Jesus' sinless perfection is, of course, His perfect, potent God-consciousness, an absolutely pure connection to that which is the universal human ideal. And it is this awareness of the universal human ideal that He (somehow) communicates to His followers, even to all people. Schleiermacher explains that Jesus' God-consciousness is communicated to humanity through belief in Him, which is also belief that the universal human ideal has made its way into real human experience: "to believe that Jesus was the Christ, and to believe that the Kingdom of God (that is the new corporate life which was to be created by God) has come, are the same thing. Consequently, all developing blessedness has its grounding in this corporate life."[68] Thus, redemption comes by way of the community that Jesus founded, which takes its influence from Jesus' example and represents the universal human ideal spreading throughout human existence and transforming human history. Note that *this* is the saving work of Christ, this founding of a Kingdom and influential example of love

---

[67] Schleiermacher, *Christian Faith*, 361.
[68] Schleiermacher, *Christian Faith*, 360.

perpetuated by this Kingdom-fellowship is how Jesus "saves" humanity.

This is a significant departure from historic Christian orthodoxy, which orients the saving work of Christ around His death on the Cross, rather than simply His life of love. Schleiermacher did not understand Jesus' death as the moment where God objectively dealt with the penalty of sin, but instead viewed the cross event as an example of self-denying love exhibited in suffering at the hands of the state. He doesn't eliminate the cross, but he does redefine it. Jesus' death is a *modeling* death, not an *atoning* death. In what will become a consistent theological pattern over the next several generations of liberalism, the life of Jesus is more significant than the death of Jesus, where even His death is simply the culmination of His life. As Schleiermacher argues, "For in His suffering unto death, occasioned by His steadfastness, there is manifested to us an absolutely self-denying love."[69] He goes on to say, "in this there is represented to us with perfect vividness the way in which God was in Him to reconcile the world to Himself," mainly through His self-sacrificing love, which was the culmination of cruciform *living*.

While emphasizing the cruciformity of Jesus' life is a good thing, even with regards to salvation, that cruciform life saves insofar as it provides a prototype for living the universal human ideal. It is this cruciformity—both the living and dying examples of love—that we are to share in order to overcome the sin of the world: "Those who are assumed into

---

[69] Schleiermacher, *Christian Faith*, 458.

the fellowship of Christ's life are called to share the fellowship of His suffering, until the time when sin has been completely overcome and through suffering satisfaction has been made in the corporate life of humanity."[70] This is the nature and purpose of the Kingdom: it is a corporation, fellowship, community from among the human race in history who, under Christ's influence, are living out His loving example, in order to transform society in to the image of the universal human ideal. As an "example" and the human "ideal,"[71] Christ's influential life functions as the mechanism by which that transformation is possible; the Kingdom is the community that perpetuates and spreads that influential life through human history, in order that "Thy will be done on earth as in heaven." Through the Kingdom of God, then, humanity finds salvation.

THE SALVATION OF THE KINGDOM

Though Schleiermacher is credited with reintroducing the concept and language of the Kingdom of God into the Church's vernacular, he defines it in a new, different way for his modern context. Schleiermacher uses various terms to represent the Kingdom of God: it is a new corporate life founded by Jesus;[72] it is fellowship with Christ, as such fellowship is always fellowship with his Kingdom mission;[73]

---

[70] Schleiermacher, *Christian Faith*, 461.

[71] Schleiermacher, *Christian Faith*, 462.

[72] Schleiermacher, *Christian Faith*, 444.

[73] Schleiermacher, *Christian Faith*, 517.

REIMAGINING THE KINGDOM

it is a special divine activity in the world;[74] the Kingdom is the Church itself;[75] it is the sphere of Christ's redeeming activity;[76] in its most basic sense the Kingdom of God is the realm in which the God-consciousness is active;[77] ultimately, it is the union of Divine essence with human nature, the reunion of ideal human essence with real human existence.[78] The founding of the Kingdom, then, is the principal work of Christ and the way in which He solves our human problem.

The Kingdom of God is the vehicle through which human nature is transformed and redeemed; the community of Jesus mediates His influence and the redeeming activity of the Kingdom throughout human history in order to change it. That influence is, of course, Jesus' powerful, potent God-consciousness that manifested itself in His powerful, potent loving model of the universal human ideal. That loving life example was perpetuated through founding the Kingdom and calling people to its redeeming mission. As Schleiermacher states, "We are conscious of all approximations to the state of blessedness which occur in the Christian life as being grounded in a new divinely-effected corporate life, which works in opposition to the corporate life of sin and the misery which develops in it."[79] Salvation, or the "state of blessedness" is rooted in the new corporate life of the

---

[74] Schleiermacher, *Christian Faith*, 552.

[75] Schleiermacher, *Christian Faith*, 528.

[76] Schleiermacher, *Christian Faith*, 530.

[77] Schleiermacher, *Christian Faith*, 43.

[78] Schleiermacher, *Christian Faith*, 738, 739.

[79] Schleiermacher, *Christian Faith*, 358.

Kingdom of God. Such salvation happens when our lives correspond to the Kingdom-life established by Jesus, when our life is seized by the living example of Jesus. As Schleiermacher explains, "Assumption into living fellowship with Christ is his justification;" conversion is regarded as a changed form of living. [80]

This assumption and conversion does not happen all at once, but rather intermittently: "the true life of Christ in us announces itself at first only in weak and intermittent impulses, and then gradually a unified activity emerges. The only marks we can point to are steady progress in sanctification taken in its full meaning, and active participation in the extension of Christ's Kingdom."[81] The "life of Christ" of which Schleiermacher speaks is not the actual presence of the resurrected Christ living in us, but the example of Jesus' life as perpetuated in the Kingdom of God and its activity. Schleiermacher writes, "the life of Christ in us is nothing but activity in behalf of the Kingdom of God which embraces men all together in the grasp of love flowing from Him; that is it is the power of the Christian common spirit."[82] This "Christian common spirit" is nothing more than the personal influence of Christ—His "Divine Essence," His God-consciousness—living on through the Church outward to humanity. And this perpetuated personal influence of Christ, the life of Christ living in us through the loving activity of the Kingdom of God, is the actual salvific

---

[80] Schleiermacher, *Christian Faith*, 478.

[81] Schleiermacher, *Christian Faith*, 516.

[82] Schleiermacher, *Christian Faith*, 576-577.

work of Jesus' redemption.[83] The salvation of humanity, then, is bound up with our extension of the Kingdom of God through acts of love by loving both God and neighbor. Here, there is a social link between the God-consciousness and love, and Kingdom salvation.

In order to understand how the Kingdom saves humanity through acts of love, it is important to note the social connection between this love and *God-consciousness*. Schleiermacher was interested in helping people reconnect to the universal ideal, which seems to be symbolized by *God*. Some have noted a panentheistic (even pantheistic) dimension to Schleiermacher's understanding of God.[84] Several times Schleiermacher invokes Spinoza's moniker "the One in All, and All in One."[85] Though he does distinguish between God and the world,[86] it is clear the All and the One cannot be separated: "The Absolute Causality to which the feeling of absolute dependence points back can only be described in such a way that, on the one hand, it is distinguished from the content of the natural order and thus contrasted with it, and, on the other hand, equated with it in comprehension."[87] John Cooper translates Schleiermacher's motto as evidence of his panentheism: "There is no God without the world, just as there is no world without God."[88]

---

[83] Schleiermacher, *Christian Faith*, 577.

[84] Cooper, *Panentheism*, 88.

[85] Schleiermacher, *On Religion*, 7.

[86] Schleiermacher, *Christian Faith*, 39: "God and the world will remain distinct at least as regards to function."

[87] Schleiermacher, *Christian Faith*, 200.

[88] Cooper, *Panentheism*, 84.

Schleiermacher's Grammar

Thus, God and humanity are intimately wrapped up in Schleiermacher's *God-consciousness* language. In fact, he uses the language of *Whole* when discussing humanity's relationship to God, where individuals compose the Whole: "Every form, every creature, every occurrence is an action of the Universe upon us, and religion is just the acceptance of each separate thing as part of the Whole, of each limited thing as an exhibition of the Infinite."[89] In light of this panentheistic connection between humanity and God, note the social link in Schleiermacher's *God-consciousness*: When I love God, I love the Whole; when I love the Whole I love my neighbor. Thus, love of neighbor actually *is* love of God. When one loves their neighbor, they are loving and affirming the universal human ideal, and consequently living the life of the Kingdom and perpetuating its activity.

Schleiermacher maintains that the true nature of the activity of the Kingdom is love: "love to men and love to Christ and love to God."[90] This love is the love of Christ's life-example living in us and our community of faith; the activity of the Kingdom is "Christ's love working in and through us."[91] Therefore, the activity of the Kingdom of God involves living out the loving example of Christ through acts of love, which is an affirmation of the universal human ideal. This

---

[89] Schleiermacher, *On Religion*, 279. In commenting on the self-existence of every individual he wrote: "What is it merely as act, as movement? Is it not the coming into being of something for itself, and at the same time in the Whole? It is an endeavor to return into the Whole, and to exist for oneself at the same time...Your whole life is such an existence for self in the Whole." Schleiermacher, *On Religion*, 42-43.

[90] Schleiermacher, *Christian Faith*, 521.

[91] Schleiermacher, *Christian Faith*, 521.

activity of the Kingdom is the activity of the Redeemer (i.e. Jesus Christ) Himself, because "the original activity of the Redeemer," Schleiermacher writes, is "that by means which he assumes us into this fellowship of His activity and His life."[92] By definition, then, the activity of love that we perform is an extension of the activity of Jesus Christ, because His activity of Redemption is our activity of love. As Schleiermacher goes on to say, "It is scarcely thinkable that a man should be received into unity of life with Christ without very soon actively proving himself an instrument of his redeeming activity."[93] Assumption into the life of Christ and His community means assuming His redeeming activity by being taken up into Christ's vocation of love. Christ's own vocation is bound up with His will for the Kingdom of God and transformation of human history through loving good works. For Schleiermacher, any loving work is good because it reflects the loving vocation of Christ, and every good work necessarily lies within the sphere of the Kingdom of God.[94] Therefore, whatever activity that reflects the loving life-example of Christ is activity that is part of the Kingdom of God. Schleiermacher has everybody in view here, because Christ's love works in and through every good work that comports with the will of the Kingdom.[95] In the end, everybody's loving activity will be considered Kingdom

---

[92] Schleiermacher, *Christian Faith*, 165.
[93] Schleiermacher, *Christian Faith*, 516.
[94] Schleiermacher, *Christian Faith*, 522.
[95] Schleiermacher, *Christian Faith*, 521.

activity because all people will eventually become members of it, which cashes out as universalism.

While Schleiermacher did equate the Church with the Kingdom and those who have faith in Christ as members of it, his reformulation of election and divine foreknowledge ultimately includes everyone as members of the Kingdom. Schleiermacher insists that those currently outside the fellowship of Christ—meaning those who do not consciously or willfully identify with Him—will go on to become members of the Church, because as they advance in Kingdom-acts of love, this "leaves no doubt as to their justification."[96] He assumes that "all belonging to the human race are eventually taken up into living fellowship with Christ, because of what he called "a single divine fore-ordination." While the majority of humanity is not yet regarded as chosen and elected in Christ, the person whose fore-ordination has not yet been fulfilled during this life is held in reserve in death in an "intermediate state," where he will eventually be "taken up into living fellowship with Christ."[97] Schleiermacher put it even more plainly when he argued, "There is a single divine fore-ordination, according to which the totality of the new creation is called into being out of the general mass of the human race," to which he then added "the totality of the new creation is equal to the general

---

[96] Schleiermacher, *Christian Faith*, 547, 549

[97] Schleiermacher, *Christian Faith*, 549. Though Schleiermacher is vague in his description of the afterlife—he is unclear what he means by "taken up into living fellowship with Christ"—it seems as though Schleiermacher held a sort of post-mortem universal salvation, in which even after death everyone will experience salvation. Even then, however, it isn't clear that Schleiermacher even held a view of an actual everlasting life of heaven post-death.

mass," so that the redeeming power of Christ saves from common ruin the totality of the new creation contained in the human race.[98] Thus, the redeeming activity of Christ (i.e. the Kingdom of God) is universal, not simply in opportunity but in outcome, so that the Kingdom of God is formed out of "the whole actual inward manifold of the human race in space and time."[99] All who belong to the human race are eventually taken up into living fellowship with Christ in the Kingdom and experience the essence of the universal human ideal that is divine love, by nature of the historical transformation of society through the advancement of the Kingdom. Schleiermacher's solution to the human problem is truly a universal salvation.

CONCLUSION

In the end, Schleiermacher conceives of the human problem relating to our failure as individuals, and collectively as humans, to live up to our greatest human potential, an ideal common spirit of brotherly love. This impairment of the universal human ideal is a historical phenomenon that demands a historical solution. This solution came in the historical person of Jesus of Nazareth, who had a potent connection to the universal human ideal and established a community of people who would carry forth His inspiring example of love through the Kingdom of God. The Kingdom is the movement of love-inspired action to help humanity grow beyond their sensuous-consciousness to live fully within

---

[98] Schleiermacher, *Christian Faith*, 550, 551.
[99] Schleiermacher, *Christian Faith*, 555.

their God-consciousness, to bring about the universal human ideal in human existence. When one loves his neighbor, he loves God because He is in All and All are in Him; love of brother is an affirmation of the universal human ideal. As one progresses through this historical theological comparison, one will notice how subsequent generations of German liberals continued Schleiermacher's *Kingdom* grammar and problem/solution formulation, even though they revised and extended his arguments along the way. Chief among those revisers and extenders was Schleiermacher's successor, Albrecht Ritschl.

REIMAGINING THE KINGDOM

CHAPTER 3
Ritschl's Grammar

Though Schleiermacher is credited with founding modern Protestant theology and fathering Protestant liberalism, Albrecht Ritschl became virtually synonymous with liberalism, founding a school and influencing a generation of theologians.[1] With the publication of the English translation of his magnum opus, *The Christian Doctrine of Justification and Reconciliation*, in 1900, Ritschl's influence grew in width and depth beyond the dominance he had already achieved in German theological discourse.[2] This influence would extend through Harnack, Rauschenbusch, and Tillich; one even finds vestiges of his school in the contemporary Emergent Church through thinkers such as McLaren. It is no wonder that Ritschl has been called the "most important Protestant theologian of the last [19th]

---

[1] Grenz and Olson, *20th Century Theology*, 53.

[2] Livingston, *Modern Christian Thought*, 247.

century after Schleiermacher."³ Ritschl's influence upon several generations of theologians has come primarily through his revision and extension of Schleiermacher's *Kingdom* grammar. For Ritschl, humanity's problem is individual selfishness, a collective social consciousness that compels us to do evil, and a rejection of the universal human ideal. As the founder of the higher common good and universal ideal of the Kingdom of God, Jesus conquered bad human existence by founding, living, and teaching this Kingdom of love, which is the source of our salvation.

RITSCHL'S HISTORICAL CONTEXT

Ritschl was born a generation after Schleiermacher, yet he still experienced the cultural and ecclesiastical effects of the Enlightenment. Early in his academic development Ritschl was influenced by C. F. Bauer and the German idealism of G. W. F. Hegel, though Ritschl later rejected both the radical left wing Hegelianism of Feurerbach and the orthodox speculative Hegelianism of the right.⁴ He was, however, heavily influenced by two 18th and 19th century thinkers: Kant and Schleiermacher.

Unlike Schleiermacher, who attempted to overcome the Enlightenment by way of Romanticism, Karl Barth explains that Ritschl "energetically seized upon the theoretical and practical philosophy of the Enlightenment in its perfected

---

³ David L. Mueller, *An Introduction to the Theology of Albrecht Ritschl* (Philadelphia: Westminster Press, 1969), 15.

⁴ Mueller, *Introduction to the Theology of Albrecht Ritschl*, 17.

Ritschl's Grammar

form. That is, he went back to Kant."[5] Grenz and Olson maintain that Ritschl's theological method was harmonious and consistent with Kant's philosophy: "Ritschl followed Kant in trying to expunge metaphysics from theology and in bringing religion into the closest possible connection with ethics."[6] Germane to this examination is the interesting note that Ritschl drew upon Kant's vision of the Kingdom as an ethical community where everyone is ruled by the highest moral virtue. As Derek Nelson explains, "Kant's vision of the Kingdom of God presented an ethical community wherein all people were perfectly ruled by virtue and the power of their consciences."[7] Rather than rooting ethics in the knowledge of God, Kant rooted ethics in the knowledge of the universal human ideal. For Kant, it is impossible to know God and His way and to have a moral faith rooted in the knowledge of God as defined by religious faith. Therefore, all that remains is to know and serve your neighbor through simple moral virtue that's rooted in the common moral good. Nelson goes on to explain that "Kant positively links this notion [of the common moral good] to the development of a 'moral faith' from the then regnant so-called 'ecclesiastical faith.' If this were to happen, according to Kant, then we could say that 'the Kingdom of God has come unto us.'"[8] And Kant's notion of this "kingdom of ends" impacted

---

[5] Karl Barth, *Protestant Thought: From Rousseau to Ritschl* (New York: Harper and Brothers, 1959), 391.

[6] Grenz and Olson, *20th Century Theology*, 55.

[7] Nelson, "Schleiermacher and Ritschl on Individual and Social Sin," 145.

[8] Nelson, "Schleiermacher and Ritschl on Individual and Social Sin,", 145.

REIMAGINING THE KINGDOM

Ritschl's own *Kingdom* grammar and concept of sin by provoking him to root both in Kant's idea of the highest common good. Furthermore, in adopting Kant's moral vision of the Kingdom, Ritschl also adopted Kant's theory of knowledge that suited the requirements of his own theological system and epistemic proof for God's existence. James Orr explains:

> That our knowledge is only of phenomena; that God is theoretically incognoscible; that our conviction of His existence rests on a practical, not on a theoretical judgment...The Kantian 'moral' proof for the existence of God Ritschl accepts as alone valid; and with it he adopts the Kantian deduction of the Kingdom of God, or association of men through laws of virtue, and the idea of a final end of the world thence resulting.[9]

Whereas Schleiermacher sought to move beyond the impasses created by the Enlightenment by pursuing an alternative route through Romanticism, Ritschl was attracted to Kant's ethics and certain forms of Neo-Kantianism.[10] Beyond Kant, however, undoubtedly the most significant impact upon Ritschl's theology was Schleiermacher.

Ritschl's feelings toward Schleiermacher ranged from attraction to repulsion. Orr explains that what "chiefly repelled Ritschl to Schleiermacher was the element of 'mysticism' in his theology; that which attracted him was, above all, his teleological view of Christianity, and the place

---

[9] James Orr, *The Ritschlian Theology and the Evangelical Faith* (London: Houghton and Stoughton, 1897), 5-6.

[10] Mueller, *Introduction to the Theology of Albrecht Ritschl*, 17.

given to the idea of 'fellowship' in religion."[11] This "teleological view" in Schleiermacher's *Kingdom* grammar refers to the end goal toward which Christianity is oriented and the end toward which humanity is called to move. While he appreciated how Schleiermacher restored the Kingdom-concept to its rightful, central place in Christian theology, Ritschl did not believe Schleiermacher went far enough in making it part of his ethic; Ritschl sought to make the Kingdom both a religious *and* ethical concept.[12] We have already seen that for Schleiermacher, the Kingdom was primarily an individual religious feeling of absolute dependence and relationship with God, the universal ideal. As Claude Welch explains, "Schleiermacher first identified the teleological character of the kingdom as decisive for Christianity. For this we should be grateful. Yet the significance of this discovery of the ethical had not been fully exploited. That was the task Ritschl set for himself."[13] While Ritschl displays fealty to Schleiermacher when he notes that the Christian redemptive end is presupposed by Schleiermacher's religious "dependence on God," he also transcends Schleiermacher's "general form of religious experience as distinct from a moral relationship" by arguing that the Christian life is both "perfectly religious and

---

[11] Orr, *The Ritschlian Theology*, 42.

[12] Nelson, "Schleiermacher and Ritschl on Individual and Social Sin," 145.

[13] Claude Welch, *Protestant Thought in the Nineteenth Century* (2 vols.: Eugene, OR: Wipf & Stock Publishers, 2003) 2:18.

perfectly ethical."[14] Schleiermacher established the foundation for such religious and ethical redemption by emphasizing the individual's loving feeling for God and neighbor through loving the Whole: in loving God I love the Whole, in loving the Whole I love my neighbor. Ritschl built on this foundation by emphasizing one's ethical posture before all humanity with his *Kingdom* grammar, the first part of which we now turn in order to understand the problem for which the Kingdom solves.

THE PROBLEM FOR WHICH THE KINGDOM SOLVES

Significant to Ritschl's understanding of the human problem is his rejection of the historic doctrine of original sin. Ritschl relegated original sin to the sphere of "doctrine," merely an intellectual idea which does not conform to experience.[15] As with Schleiermacher, Ritschl rejected the notion that our original parents historically fell from an original righteousness.[16] Ritschl challenged the doctrine of original sin that developed in the early church by insisting that it simply does not reflect the New Testament: "Neither Jesus nor any of the New Testament writers either indicate or presuppose that sin is universal merely through natural generation."[17] Likewise, he disputed as unbiblical the

---

[14] Albrecht Ritschl, *The Christian Doctrine of Justification and Reconciliation: The Positive Development of the Doctrine*. Edited by H.R. Mackintosh and A.B. Macaulay (Edinburgh: T & T Clark, 1902.), 13.

[15] Ritschl, *Justification and Reconciliation*, 328.

[16] Ritschl, *Justification and Reconciliation*, 331.

[17] Ritschl, *Instruction in the Christian Religion*, 203.n27.

Ritschl's Grammar

Reformed assertion that humans are incapable of doing good because of their inherent sinfulness.[18] Furthermore, Ritschl argued that original sin is neither derived from the natural endowment of man[19] nor inherited from previous generations.[20] Instead, Ritschl argued that sin is acquired through human history and development.

He asserted that the generations from our first human parents became trapped in an avalanche of crises that engulfed humanity in ethically dysfunctional systems and destructive stories, resulting in a "selfish bias." According to Ritschl, humanity is now caught in a "whole web of sinful actions and reactions, which presuppose and yet again increases the selfish bias in every man."[21] Humans were originally created with the capacity to freely choose the highest or the "perfect common good."[22] From the beginning humans possessed an internal goodness, and out of that goodness they were to act in accordance with the highest common good, which the Kingdom of God now reflects. However, our problem is that we are caught in webs of ethically dysfunctional systems and destructive stories that have escalated throughout human history. Our problem is not a natural, internal one—in that I am born a rebel against God and the object of His righteous wrath, in need of a rescuer—but an environmental, external one: I follow the bad

---

[18] Ritschl, *Instruction in the Christian Religion*, 206-207.n4.

[19] Ritschl, *Instruction in the Christian Religion*, 204.

[20] Ritschl, *Justification and Reconciliation*, 348.

[21] Ritschl, *Justification and Reconciliation*, 350.

[22] Ritschl, *Instruction in the Christian Religion*, 202.

ethical examples around me and do ethically bad things, and need someone to show me how to live my best life now. Accordingly, *I* am not the problem; *life* and my environment is the problem, and I respond with more bad actions. Thus, Ritschl has a Pelagian view of original sin and human nature.

Ritschl defines sin in several ways: In content, sin is selfishness; in form, it is enmity toward God, a mistrust and indifference toward Him; in origin, it arises out of ignorance, bad examples, and habit.[23] Ritschl's definitions gain steam when he interprets sin through the lens of the Kingdom of God. Taking his cues from Schleiermacher, Ritschl posits a *kingdom of sin*[24] set over against the Kingdom of God in which all humanity shares in its guilt: "All these grades of habitual sin we include in the vast complexity of sinful action when we form the idea of the *kingdom of sin*...we can only regard ourselves as sharing its guilt when we not only attribute to ourselves our own sinful action as such, but at the same time calculate how they produce sin in others also..."[25] The subject of sin is not simply individuals who do selfish acts that run contrary to the highest common good (i.e. the Kingdom of the God), but instead "is *humanity as the sum of all individuals*, in so far as the selfish action of each person...is directed in any degree whatsoever towards the opposite of the good, and leads to the association of individuals in common

---

[23] Ritschl, *Justification and Reconciliation*, 334-336.

[24] In *Justification and Reconciliation*, 339, Ritschl acknowledges the merit of Schleiermacher's *common sin* equation, though believed he wrongly subsumed it under the traditional heading of original sin. Instead, Ritschl substituted the idea of the *kingdom of sin* in place of original sin.

[25] Ritschl, *Justification and Reconciliation*, 338.

evil."[26] Thus, I and my sin nature are not the problem; humanity and the environment it creates is the problem.

For Ritschl, the *kingdom of sin* is an alternative hypothesis to original sin that explains the human condition.[27] While the doctrine of original sin views Adam's sin as a nature-altering act, Ritschl views Adam's sin as an *environment*-altering act. In Adam, there is a universal loss of connection, dependence, reverence, and trust in God, because every generation has actively participated in the transgression of freely mistrusting God and rejecting the perfect moral good, the universal human ideal. These collective acts have resulted in the *kingdom of sin* or "web of sin," which is set over against the Kingdom of God. This kingdom or universal sinfulness is the collective human sinfulness that acts as a collective consciousness out of which individuals act. Ritschl describes this kingdom and universality as "united action" which leads to a reinforcement of sin in every generation: "United sin, this opposite of the kingdom of God, rests upon all as a power which at least limits the freedom of the individual to do good."[28] The sin that swirls around us compels us to sin, resulting in a sinful bias that individuals acquire because of bad examples. Ritschl explains, "The sinful bias…is not described by [Paul] as inherited, and can with perfect reason be understood as something acquired. In the individual [the sinful bias] comes to be the principle of the will's direction."[29]

---

[26] Ritschl, *Justification and Reconciliation*, 335.

[27] Ritschl, *Justification and Reconciliation*, 344.

[28] Ritschl, *Instruction in the Christian Religion*, 206.

[29] Ritschl, *Justification and Reconciliation*, 346, 347.

This individual bias contributes to the larger whole of "wickedness and untruth" in what Ritschl terms a "web of sinful action." It is the collective contribution of individual actions and reactions and also "increases the selfish bias in every man."[30]

Ritschl believed our human problem is what we do and not who we are by nature—we do not sin because we're sinners; we are a sinner because we sin in concert with humanity and its web of sin. The web of sin that surrounds us creates a bias within us toward selfishness and compels us to sin; we are oppressed on the outside not affected on the inside. Therefore, our solution must address this evil web of systems, the person who came to bring us that solution had to do something with that web. We didn't need a savior to stand in our place of punishment; we needed someone to launch a better system, a better Kingdom. As Barth explains Ritschl's position, solving our human problem means "the realized ideal of human life."[31] Jesus was such a person who provided such a solution by living such an ideal human life.

THE BEARER OF THE KINGDOM: THE PERSON AND WORK OF JESUS

Like other generations of liberal theologians, Ritschl's understanding of Jesus plays a significant role in Ritschl's *Kingdom* grammar. How Ritschl understands and interprets the person of Jesus has great bearing on how he understands His work, and thus the solution found in the Kingdom of

---

[30] Ritschl, *Justification and Reconciliation*, 350.

[31] Barth, *Protestant Thought*, 393.

Ritschl's Grammar

God to humanity's problem. Whereas Schleiermacher tended to make Jesus out to be simply a religious figure who solved our religious problem—mainly, our God-forgetfulness—Ritschl emphasized both the religious and ethical aspects of the "Founder of Christianity." For Ritschl, "Jesus, the Founder of the perfect moral and spiritual religion, belongs to a higher order than all other men;" "His unique worth lies in the manner in which He mastered His spiritual powers through a self-consciousness which transcends that of all other men..."[32] As a uniquely higher man, He was "conscious of a new and hitherto unknown relation to God."[33] Here we see great continuity with Schleiermacher's own understanding of Jesus, who he said had a potent God-consciousness, a perfect feeling of absolute connection with and relation to God (i.e. the universal human ideal). Similarly, Ritschl does not describe Jesus as being God himself; Jesus is only a unique *man* belonging to a higher order of humanity. In regard to this relationship with God, Jesus is described as having a *"strength of a fellowship or unity with God* such as no one before Him had ever known."[34] Ritschl did not suggest Jesus is ontologically one with God, but that He simply has a unique relationship with Him as demonstrated in His ethical life.

Like Schleiermacher, Ritschl does not indicate that Jesus Himself is God, only that He shows us the Divine and has a connection with the Divine. Christ's ethical actions are what

---

[32] Ritschl, *Justification and Reconciliation*, 2, 332.

[33] Ritschl, *Justification and Reconciliation*, 386.

[34] Ritschl, *Justification and Reconciliation*, 333. (emphasis mine.)

connect Him to God and give Jesus what Ritschl termed the Godhead attribute. As Ritschl explains, "Christ's Godhead is understood as the power which Christ has put forth for our redemption...[the Godhead attribute] of Christ is to be found in the service He provided, the benefit He bestows, the saving work He accomplishes...it is an attribute revealed to us in His saving influence upon ourselves."[35] In other words, Jesus of Nazareth is God because of what He *does,* not because of *who He is.* Jesus is not ontologically God, but onlyethically so: He only shares in the Divine because of His ethical services and actions, rather than being God Himself. For Ritschl Jesus is the *moral* rather than the *metaphysical* Son of God.

As Ritschl makes clear, it is in the ethical activity of Jesus that we find God present. While Ritschl does say "[Jesus] is equal to God," it is clear from his writings that this equality is ethical, rather than ontological. He is equal with God because of His moral activity.[36] This activity is primarily the fulfillment of His vocation as the founder of the Kingdom. "Vocation" is another concept for which Ritschl is indebted to Schleiermacher. As Ritschl says, Jesus is the "personal vehicle of the Divine self-end;" He is "that Being in the world Whose self-end God makes effective and manifest after the original manner His own eternal self-end, Whose whole activity, therefore, in discharge of His vocation, forms the material of that complete revelation of God which is present in Him, in Whom, in short, the Word of God is a human

---

[35] Ritschl, *Justification and Reconciliation*, 395, 396-397, 398.

[36] Ritschl, *Justification and Reconciliation*, 483.

person."³⁷ Jesus reveals God through His vocation as the founder of the Kingdom of God, as a "teacher" and "liver" of the "universal ethical kingdom of God," which is the "supreme end of God Himself in the world."³⁸ Jesus' ethical teachings and kingdom vocation, then, constitute Him as participating in the Divine "Godhead." Understanding the person of Jesus in His vocation as the Founder of the Kingdom provides the needed theological context for understanding the work of Jesus, what He did in that vocation.

Because the realization of the universal human ideal is the manner in which our human problem is solved, the nature of Jesus' work must be refashioned and re-understood. Rather than conceiving that reconciling, solving work happening at Jesus' death on the cross, Ritschl believed that work centered upon His life, a life that simply climaxed at the cross. Insofar as Jesus' work is re-understood as centering around His Kingdom-vocation, so too is the cross itself. This re-understanding is different than historic Christianity that views the cross as the event at which Jesus Christ went to sacrifice Himself for our sins in our place as a vicarious substitute. Ritschl maintained this view is patently unbiblical and instead is a principle of Hellenic religion.³⁹ As with Schleiermacher before him, Ritschl rejected the traditional substitutionary view of the cross that provides the solution to our human problem of sin: "The view that Christ, by the

---

³⁷ Ritschl, *Justification and Reconciliation*, 451.

³⁸ Ritschl, *Justification and Reconciliation*, 451.

³⁹ Ritschl, *Justification and Reconciliation*, 478.

vicarious endurance of the punishment deserved by sinful men, propitiated the justice or wrath of God, and thus made possible the grace of God, is not found on any clear and distinct passage in the New Testament."[40] Ritschl did not believe the solution to man's problem of alienation comes through the substitution of Christ on the cross. Instead, he argued that the significance of Jesus' work on the cross was simply a continuation or climax of His life. For him the cross served as an example to the rest of the world: "It is not mere fate of dying that determines the value of Christ's death as a sacrifice; what renders this issue of his life significant for others is His willing acceptance of the death inflicted on Him by His adversaries as a dispensation of God, and the highest proof of faithfulness to His vocation."[41] In other words, as with Schleiermacher, Jesus is important not because He *died* —as a substitutionary sacrifice for the sins of the world—but because He *lived*; salvation comes through the *life* of Christ in executing His vocation as founder of the Kingdom.

The significance of the work of Jesus is "'related to the moral organization of humanity through love-prompted action,"[42] the Kingdom of God. His vocation was founding, living, and teaching the love-prompted actions of the Kingdom, providing the means by which humanity can triumph over and transcend the ethically bad systems of the world. Through this vocation He provided the paradigmatic example of self-sacrifice, discipline, and attainment of virtue

---

[40] Ritschl, *Instruction in the Christian Religion*, 220.n3.

[41] Ritschl, *Justification and Reconciliation*, 477, 479

[42] Ritschl, *Justification and Reconciliation*, 13.

Ritschl's Grammar

for others to follow, which crescendoed at the cross. The cross was an extension of Jesus' life in that His sufferings served as a means of testing His faithfulness to His Kingdom vocation, while also confirming and explaining it.[43] For Ritschl, the work of Christ did not center on the cross, but on founding, living, and teaching the Kingdom; the cross was the culmination of that vocation in that this highest ethical common good was tested and displayed for all the world to see and follow. In this testing and display, humans find their moral example to aid their moral failure and their solution to their problem of selfishness and dominion over bad existence, which is the Kingdom of God, the true nature of Christ's work.

Ritschl explicitly argues that the Kingdom of God "offers the solution to the question...implied in all religions: namely, how man, recognizing himself as a part of the world, and at the same time as being capable of a spiritual personality, can attain that dominion over the world, as opposed to limitation by it, which this capability gives him the right to claim."[44] Mirroring Schleiermacher's own view of the human predicament Ritschl wondered how humanity could attain dominion over and conquer the limitations of human existence? Humanity's limited human existence is conquered through attaining the universal human ideal found in the Kingdom of God, which is the end toward which all of humanity is to move because it is the supreme end of God

---

[43] Ritschl, *Justification and Reconciliation*, 480.
[44] Ritschl, *Instruction in the Christian Religion*, 179.

Himself.⁴⁵ Attaining the ethical ideal of the Kingdom is possible through the justification and reconciliation Christ provides, which are really one in the same.

While others often separate justification and the Kingdom of God, claiming that "justification and reconciliation concern men as sinners, while the Kingdom of God concerns them as reconciled," Ritschl insisted this dichotomy is "not quite exact."⁴⁶ Instead, "the conception of the Kingdom of God and justification are homogeneous," for they are one and the same idea.⁴⁷ The aim of justification and reconciliation is "lordship over the world" in order to transcend the systems and stories of human existence through "dominion over the world and participation in the Kingdom of God."⁴⁸ As Ritschl defines reconciliation: "[it] is not merely the ground of deliverance from the guilt of sin...it is also the ground of deliverance from the world, and the ground of spiritual and moral lordship over the world."⁴⁹ Rather than deliverance from the *condition* of sin, we receive deliverance from the *effects* of sin. This conclusion seems to be established through Ritschl's claims that justification leads to eternal life now, "which is present in our experiences of freedom or lordship over the world, and in the independence of self-feeling both from the restrictions and from the impulses due to natural causes or particular sections of

---

⁴⁵ Ritschl, *Justification and Reconciliation*, 451.
⁴⁶ Ritschl, *Justification and Reconciliation*, 31.
⁴⁷ Ritschl, *Justification and Reconciliation*, 33.
⁴⁸ Ritschl, *Justification and Reconciliation*, 609, 628.
⁴⁹ Ritschl, *Justification and Reconciliation*, 357.

society."⁵⁰ Rather than the person of Jesus and His work on the cross, the Kingdom itself is the mode of salvation. Jesus saves only insofar as He brings in the Kingdom, rather than His own meritorious work on the cross. Thus, it could be said that the *Kingdom*, rather than *Jesus*, is what saves.

THE SALVATION OF THE KINGDOM

Ritschl described the Kingdom of God in various ways: "The kingdom of God is the divinely vouched-for highest good of the community;"⁵¹ it is the community of people who "are knit together in union with everyone who can show the marks of a neighbor," who do good in the Christian sense, which is the "uninterrupted reciprocation of action springing from the motive of love;"⁵² finally, "it is that union of men in which all good are appropriated in their proper subordination to the highest good."⁵³ As Ritschl plainly put it, the Kingdom of God is the product of "love-inspired action" and "the righteous conduct in which the members of the Christian community share in the bringing in of the kingdom of God [which] has its universal law and its personal motive in love to God and to one's neighbor."⁵⁴ The Kingdom is not the eschatological reign of God per se that will restore the world from the consequences of sin, but rather the "moral society of nations" and ultimately "the

---

⁵⁰ Ritschl, *Justification and Reconciliation*, 534-534.

⁵¹ Ritschl, *Instruction in the Christian Religion*, 174.

⁵² Ritschl, *Justification and Reconciliation*, 334.

⁵³ Ritschl, *Justification and Reconciliation*, 451.

⁵⁴ Ritschl, *Instruction in the Christian Religion*, 178, 174.

organization of humanity through action inspired by love."⁵⁵ In Ritschl's *Kingdom* grammar, then, one finds community, love-motivated action, and good defined by the "highest good." This latter characteristic—the highest good—is of particular interest because it further defines the Kingdom as the "ethical ideal." The Kingdom forms "the ethical ideal for whose attainment the members of the community bind themselves together through their definite reciprocal action."⁵⁶ The members of the community are viewed as everyone who takes upon himself the ethical ideal found in the Kingdom.

In order to understand who is part of the Kingdom, one must understand that Ritschl distinguished between two separate communities that are drawn together by Jesus: the Church and the Kingdom. Contrary to Schleiermacher, Ritschl insisted that the Church is not the Kingdom, and spends a great deal of time explaining how Augustine and the Reformers were "erroneous" and ultimately "lost sight of the idea of the Kingdom of God."⁵⁷ As was previously addressed in the introduction chapter, Augustine equated the Kingdom of God with the Catholic Church and the Reformers generally viewed the Kingdom as the spiritual realm of God's worshippers and will over against that of the State. Instead of these conceptions, Ritschl insisted the Church—or more specifically "a legally constituted" church, as in a local congregation—is a *religious* idea, whereas the Kingdom is an

---

[55] Ritschl, *Justification and Reconciliation*, 10, 12.

[56] Ritschl, *Instruction in the Christian Religion*, 174-175.

[57] Ritschl, *Justification and Reconciliation*, 286.

ethical idea that's entirely distinct from the Church. As he argues, a Church is a "fellowship of Christians for the purpose of religious worship" and "its members unite in the same religious worship and create for this purpose a legal constitution."[58] The Kingdom, however, is a fellowship that "acts reciprocally from love, and thus calls into existence that fellowship of moral disposition and moral blessing which extends to the limits of the human race." This community "gives themselves to the interchange of action prompted by love."[59] Here Ritschl makes an important distinction between the *religious* and *ethical* fellowships of Jesus: the visible, religious fellowship of Christ is simply those who are part of the Christian religion, whereas the invisible, ethical fellowship is those who do moral acts prompted by love. This former category is related to the latter, yet is specific to those who confess the Christian religion; the latter category is far more general and includes everybody who performs acts of brotherly neighbor-love. Whereas Schleiermacher equated the Kingdom with the Church, Ritschl subsumes the Church underneath the Kingdom; the Church is a subset of the Kingdom, which inevitably universalizes the Kingdom to include every loving act by everybody.

Conceiving of the fellowship of Christ in these two manners means that anyone who does acts of love is part of the Kingdom, whether they specifically believe in Jesus (or even know of Him) or not. By Ritschl's definition, doing acts of love means one believes in Christ insofar as one believes in

---

[58] Ritschl, *Justification and Reconciliation*, 289, 290.

[59] Ritschl, *Justification and Reconciliation*, 289, 290.

the "ruling *idea* of Jesus"⁶⁰ by living out His example of love. As Ritschl writes, "The presence of the Kingdom...is always invisible and a matter of religious faith," but still the Kingdom "exists in the world as the present product of action motivated by love."⁶¹ Read in light of the above distinction between Church and Kingdom, it is important to note that the Kingdom is not simply present when the *Church* performs acts of love; any act of love from *anyone* counts as the presence of the Kingdom. Whereas Schleiermacher identified the Kingdom with the Church—though he still envisioned the whole human race would eventually be part of this new corporate life—Ritschl widened the scope of Kingdom activity beyond its previously narrow identification with the Church to include everyone from every culture and society that participates in the "highest good." Widening the margins of the Kingdom makes sense as Ritschl envisions the Kingdom to be the final end of everyone.

Ritschl makes it clear that the Kingdom of God is "the final end of all," which he defines as "the moral organization of humanity through love-prompted action."⁶² It is the final end of all, the end goal for which we all live, because it is the final end of God Himself.⁶³ The Kingdom rises above the

---

⁶⁰ Ritschl, *Justification and Reconciliation*, 284. Ritschl presents a sharp distinction between *moral* followers of Christ and *devotional* followers of Christ, relegating the former to the conception of the Kingdom of God who follow Jesus by nature of their moral actions and the latter to the conception of the worshipping community of the Church who follow Jesus by their devotional actions (i.e. prayer, Sunday worship, baptism, etc...).

⁶¹ Ritschl, *Instruction in the Christian Religion*, 179.

⁶² Ritschl, *Justification and Reconciliation*, 13.

⁶³ Ritschl, *Instruction in the Christian Religion*, 211.

mundane (i.e. life existence) and is "supernatural, in so far as it is higher than the ethical forms of society," because it is the "product of love-inspired action" and is "the highest good of those who are united in it."[64] This love-inspired action flows directly from God, who is Himself love. Ritschl explains:

> The Christian idea of the Kingdom of God, which has been proved the correlate of the conception of God as love, denotes the association of mankind—an association both extensively and intensively the most comprehensive possible—through the reciprocal moral action of its members, action which transcends all merely natural and particular considerations.[65]

In order to get into the Kingdom, then, one only has to direct his impulses and activity toward living out the love of God, which is instantiated in the inspiring example of Jesus. *Kingdom* is the catch-all language for describing every activity from every person that conforms to the universal human ideal originally modeled by Jesus Christ. By performing the Kingdom in following the loving example of Jesus, one finds salvation and is counted among the members of that Kingdom, making it clear that the Kingdom saves, and saves everybody.

CONCLUSION

Like Schleiermacher, Ritschl raised the profile on the Kingdom by placing it at the center of his theology. Whereas

---

[64] Ritschl, *Instruction in the Christian Religion*, 178.

[65] Ritschl, *Justification and Reconciliation*, 284.

REIMAGINING THE KINGDOM

Schleiermacher's emphasis was religious, Ritschl's was both religious and ethical. In fact, the term *Kingdom* served as the interpretive lens for his theological method. Our human problem is the *kingdom of sin*, which creates a selfish bias in individuals who form bad habits from following bad examples. For Ritschl, sin isn't part of the human nature, but is developmental and historical, in that every generation perpetuates and reinforces a collective sinful bias. Thus, our problem is an external, environmental problem in need of an environmental solution, rather than an internal one requiring a change to our sinful nature; the evil systems that compel people to do evil actions need an alternative ethical system that directs people toward the universal human ideal. That solution is found in the Kingdom of God, which is founded by Jesus Christ.

Rather than dying for our sins in order to transform our human nature, Jesus showed us and lived out the universal ethical ideal of the Kingdom. Salvation is found when a person aligns his life with Jesus' teachings and Kingdom, and participates in His own vocation of love-inspired activity. Such an alignment and participation is what transforms humanity's existence, which stands opposed to the highest ethical ideal. Thus, the Kingdom saves, rather than Jesus Himself. Ritschl's foundation catalyzed an entire theological movement, bent on re-formulating the gospel itself. Chief among this movement was Walter Rauschenbusch, architect of the so-called Social Gospel. To him we now turn.

CHAPTER 4
Rauschenbusch's Grammar

If Schleiermacher focused almost entirely on the religious aspect of the Kingdom and Ritschl emphasized both its religious and ethical nature, Rauschenbusch stressed almost exclusively the ethical. And whereas Schleiermacher and Ritschl emphasized the individual in relation to the universal human ideal, Rauschenbusch's unique contribution to liberal *Kingdom* grammar was his emphasis on the social: "The kingdom of God is the true human *society*,"[1] not simply the true human individual. This socializing of *Kingdom* grammar led Rauschenbusch to envision the gospel socially, as well— hence the so-called *social gospel*. Cornel West described Rauschenbusch as "the most influential and important religious public intellectual in early-twentieth-century

---

[1] Walter Rauschenbusch, *Christianity and the Social Crisis in the 21st Century*. (ed. Paul Rauschenbusch; New York: HaperOne, 2007), 58. (emph. mine)

America,"[2] an influence that has continued even today. Therefore, understanding his *Kingdom* grammar and how it solves the human problem of social evil and personal selfishness through the power of Christ's life will help us understand how that grammar is defined even today.

RAUSCHENBUSCH'S HISTORICAL CONTEXT

Rauschenbusch was born into a German Baptist family, falling under the influence of his professor father and his theologically conservative pietism.[3] He eventually accepted a pastorate position at Second German Baptist Church in Hell's Kitchen, one of the most impoverished slums of New York City.[4] It was in this context of mass poverty and systemic injustice that Rauschenbusch began his turn toward a social understanding of the gospel, and especially the Kingdom of God. As Gary Dorrien puts it, "His searing encounter with urban poverty, especially the funerals that he performed for children, drove him to political activism and a social-progressive understanding of Christianity."[5] It is this "social-progressive understanding of Christianity" that would result in the so-called *social gospel* and formulation of his *Kingdom* grammar in social terms.

---

[2] Cornel West, "Can These Dry Bones Live?" in *Christianity and the Social Crisis in the 21st Century*. (ed. Paul Rauschenbusch; New York: HaperOne, 2007), 231.

[3] Livingston, *Modern Christian Thought*, 262.

[4] Livingston, *Modern Christian Thought*, 262.

[5] Gary Dorrien, "Kingdom Coming: Rauschenbusch's Christianity and the Social Crisis." *Christian Century* 124 no 24 (2007): 27.

Rauschenbusch's Grammar

Whereas Schleiermacher and Ritschl attempted to connect the Christian faith to a post-Enlightenment culture skeptical of the faith's reasonableness, Rauschenbusch sought to connect the Christian faith to a post-Industrial culture skeptical of the faith's ethical viability. He wrote during a time when the modern city was hemorrhaging from the effects of economic inequity and insecurity, poor working conditions, alcoholism, immigration tensions, and other moral blights associated with modern industrial life. In response, Rauschenbusch did for American Christianity what Schleiermacher did for the European faith: He resurrected the language of the *Kingdom* from the neglect of Christian history in order to solve the "social crisis" of his day. Rather than applying the Kingdom religiously, as Schleiermacher had by emphasizing the individual's religious affections toward God, Rauschenbusch applied it ethically. This ethical emphasis most acutely arose during the time he spent studying in Germany where he came under the influence of Ritschlianism.[6]

While Rauschenbusch was theologically eclectic—drawing upon the theologies of Schleiermacher, German Idealism, and evolutionary doctrine—his major theological themes have a strong Ritschlian ring to them. Ritschl and his school dominated the European theological scene when Rauschenbusch was studying sociology and New Testament in Germany in 1891, leading some to conclude a special

---

[6] Grenz and Olson, *Twentieth Century Theology*, 61.

Ritschlian influence upon his theological outlook.[7] A generation prior, Ritschl had emphasized the ethical nature of the Kingdom and Jesus as founder of a new corporate life that centered around the highest human good. This corporate life, centering around the influential words and deeds of Jesus Himself, solved the systemic "kingdom of sin" that defines our human problem. Many of these themes found their way into Rauschenbusch's theology, especially Ritschl's preoccupation with a social-progressive understanding of the gospel and emphasis on the ethical Kingdom. Though he later parted with Ritschl's "ellipses" understanding of Christianity—while Ritschl maintained Christianity had two centers, eternal life for the individual and the Kingdom for humanity, Rauschenbusch came to believe Jesus had one center of thought, the Kingdom of God—[8] Rauschenbusch's major theological themes are extraordinarily similar to Ritschlian liberalism. As Livingston points out, "Like the Ritschlians, he was disinterested in metaphysics and dogma as the initiator of the divine community—the Kingdom of God. He saw man as caught in the struggle between his spiritual and natural impulses and conceived salvation in ethical and social terms."[9] Rauschenbusch combined these Ritschlian themes with two other important forces in American thought: evolution and socialism.

---

[7] Max L. Stackhouse, introduction to *The Righteousness of the Kingdom*, by Walter Rauschenbusch (ed. Max L. Stackhouse. New York: Abingdon Press, 1968), 18.

[8] Dorrien, "Kingdom Coming," 27.

[9] Livingston, *Modern Christian Thought*, 263.

Consistent with a Darwinian scientific perspective of the world, Rauschenbusch appealed in several of his works to the progressive, evolutionary development of humanity. He speaks of an "infinite slowness and imperfection of historical progress." He goes on to argue that for the first time in religious history humanity can direct religious energies "by scientific knowledge," knowledge that takes into account "the modern comprehension of the organic development of human society."[10] Elsewhere, Rauschenbusch makes an overtly positive assessment of evolutionary thought in relation to social change: "Evolution teaches the possibility of change for the better, not the certainty of it....The assumption that, on the whole, evolution is moving forward and upward rests partly on sight, but even more on faith."[11] This positive assessment of evolution plays a significant role in the backdrop to Rauschenbusch's *Kingdom* grammar, as does his curious assessment of socialism and communism.

Of socialism, Rauschenbusch writes, "how quickly [will] Christian thought realize that individualism is coming to be an inadequate and antiquated form of social organization which must give place to a higher form of communistic organization," adding "communism will afford a far nobler social basis for the spiritual temple of Christianity."[12] Elsewhere he writes positively that socialism itself is the answer to the social crisis facing modern industrial life, arguing that this socialistic "solution" should be "hailed with

---

[10] Rauschenbusch, *Christianity and the Social Crisis*, 164, 171, 72.

[11] Rauschenbusch, *Righteousness and the Kingdom*, 280.

[12] Rauschenbusch, *Christianity and the Social Crisis*, 320.

joy by every patriot and Christian."[13] Rauschenbusch even goes so far as to wed socialism and the Christian principle of brotherly association, which the Kingdom of God represents, as a necessary ally of the working class.[14] Understanding this socialism aspect to his historical context is important considering the words *social* and *solidaric* are key to Rauschenbusch's conception of Christianity. Socialism especially undergirds his understanding of the person and work of Jesus, the heart of whom was the message of the Kingdom, a message of social redemption and human progress.

THE PROBLEM FOR WHICH THE KINGDOM SOLVES

If Rauschenbush read traditional theological categories through a social lens, particularly the person and work of Jesus, then we should expect to find the human problem to be defined in much the same way. Rauschenbusch asserts that sin is essentially selfishness, emphasizing that it possesses ethical and social dimensions.[15] He insists that conceiving sin as selfishness "furnishes an excellent theological basis for a social conception of sin and salvation."[16] This definition works in his system because Rauschenbusch believes humanity is the object against which we sin, rather than God. He states that

---

[13] Rauschenbusch, *Christianity and the Social Crisis*, 328.

[14] Rauschenbusch, *Christianity and the Social Crisis*, 328-329.

[15] Walter Rauschenbusch, *A Theology for the Social Gospel* (Nashville: Abingdon Press, 1945), 47.

[16] Rauschenbusch, *A Theology for the Social Gospel*, 47. (emph. mine)

we sin against "our higher self, against the good of men, and against the universal good."[17] Perhaps a better way of putting it is that we sin against the universal human ideal, against the way things ought to be in human relations. While traditional theology views the human problem as "a sort of solitary duel of the will between him and God," Rauschenbusch curiously maintains that "in actual life such titanic rebellion against the Almighty is rare...We do not rebel; we dodge and evade." Instead of humanity being an enemy of God through willful sin, "The really grinding and destructive enemy of man is man."[18] In place of a theo-centric definition of sin, Rauschenbusch asserts a social, human-centric definition of sin. Sin is social because sin is selfishness. And the way we fall into selfishness is through bad examples, difficult social circumstances, and habit.

According to Rauschenbusch, we are conditioned to sin for a variety of social reasons: we are "ignorant," thus we need to be educated upward; people are placed in socially "difficult situations" that overwhelmingly tempt them beyond their capacity to resist; "evil habits of boyhood" draw us into sin, which originate "by the examples and social suasion of boys just one stage older."[19] This description of sin is obviously Pelagian, as it roots the cause of sin in ignorance, bad examples, and habit. Like Schleiermacher and Ritschl, Rauschenbusch does not conceive of our human problem in terms consistent with the historic understanding of original

---

[17] Rauschenbusch, *A Theology for the Social Gospel*, 47.

[18] Rauschenbusch, *Christianity and the Social Crisis*, 178. (emph. mine)

[19] Rauschenbusch, *A Theology for the Social Gospel*, 60, 61, 71

sin; sin is not part of our nature given to us by Adam, it is part of our nature because of our social conditioning. In classic Pelagian form he writes, "One generation corrupts the next...sin is lodged in social customs and institutions and is absorbed by the individual from his social group."[20] Our social class, profession, neighborhood, and nation compel us to sin by overtaking our moral judgments and valuations.[21] We are united in our social condition because of our sin environment, not our sin nature. And because our sin is social, so too is our guilt.

As we become more enlightened, Rauschenbusch insists we "can not help feeling a growing sense of responsibility and guilt for the common sins under which humanity is bound and to which we all contribute."[22] Rather than being individually responsible and guilty before God as a rebellious sinner against Him and His laws, we are collectively guilty because the "human spirit" as a collective whole gives itself to evil and interferes with efforts to better society.[23] As he explains, "the sin of all is in each of us,"[24] which is remarkably similar to Schleiermacher's own description that "in each the work of all and in all the work of each."[25] We are united in our sin socially; we sin because others sin and are collectively guilty because of it. This sense of social solidarity stems from

---

[20] Rauschenbusch, *A Theology for the Social Gospel*, 60.

[21] Rauschenbusch, *A Theology for the Social Gospel*, 61.

[22] Rauschenbusch, *A Theology for the Social Gospel*, 91.

[23] Rauschenbusch, *Righteousness and the Kingdom*, 282.

[24] Rauschenbusch, *A Theology for the Social Gospel*, 91.

[25] Schleiermacher, *The Christian Faith*, 288.

Rauschenbusch's concept of the Kingdom of Evil, a concept that mirrors Ritschl's kingdom of sin.

For Rauschenbusch the doctrine of the Kingdom of Evil is an important organizing concept for his understanding of sin because every human life is tightly interwoven. He writes, "The evils of one generation are caused by the wrongs of the generation that preceded, and will in turn condition the sufferings and temptations of those who come after."[26] Rauschenbusch goes on to say that "Our theological conception of sin is but fragmentary unless we see all men in their natural groups bound together in a solidarity of all times and all places, bearing the yoke of evil and suffering."[27] Rauschenbusch is careful to point out that while the concept of the Kingdom of Evil is not new, his modern conception is historical and social rather than spiritual; his concept has nothing to do with a realm of Satan and demonic spirits, but social solidarity and the historic realities of sin.[28] The agents of this theological reunderstanding are what Rauschenbusch calls "supra-personal forces." These forces are the institutions and systems of society that combine to exert their power and influence over individuals, compelling them to sin. The power of these forces results in the social sins that frustrate the Kingdom of God, resulting in social misery. At the time of Rauschenbusch, our social misery and human problem was the result of the industrial revolution and its resulting effects on land and people, work and wages, health and nutrition,

---

[26] Rauschenbusch, *A Theology for the Social Gospel*, 79.

[27] Rauschenbusch, *A Theology for the Social Gospel*, 81.

[28] Rauschenbusch, *A Theology for the Social Gospel*, 87. Also, see 81-86.

family, and democracy.[29] Perhaps today such social misery is the result of the information revolution and social fragmentation that has accompanied it. Because of this social misery, Rauschenbusch says humanity is "haunted by the horrible emptiness of his life and feels that existence is a meaningless riddle and delusion."[30] Thus, we are in need of a solution that provides a new system and way of collectively being human, one where existence is as it ought to be.

THE BEARER OF THE KINGDOM: THE PERSON AND WORK OF JESUS

Rauschenbusch insists that "the better we know Jesus, the more social do his thoughts and aims become."[31] For Rauschenbusch, Jesus was more than simply a moral teacher: He learned the greatest and deepest secret of them all: "how to live a religious life," which helps solve for the emptiness of man's life and feeling that "existence is a meaningless riddle and delusion." [32] According to Rauschenbusch, Jesus "saw the evil in the life of men and their suffering" and He wanted people "to live a right life in common."[33] This right life in common is foundational to Jesus' person and work, which centers around the "creation and progress of social redemption," the revolutionary force of the Kingdom.

---

[29] Rauschenbusch, *Christianity and the Social Crisis*, 182. See 184-230.
[30] Rauschenbusch, *Christianity and the Social Crisis*, 41.
[31] Rauschenbusch, *Christianity and the Social Crisis*, 41.
[32] Rauschenbusch, *Christianity and the Social Crisis*, 41.
[33] Rauschenbusch, *Christianity and the Social Crisis*, 41.

Like Schleiermacher and Ritschl before him, Rauschenbusch's Jesus is the founder of the Kingdom of God. He described this founding in these ways: Jesus Christ was the "initiatory power" of the Kingdom—Jesus' life set the Kingdom into motion;[34] He is the one who set in motion the historical forces of Kingdom redemption in order to overthrow the Kingdom of Evil;[35] in founding the Kingdom, Jesus "labored to set up the true standard of goodness," through His teachings and his living;[36] and finally, the Kingdom itself constitutes the fundamental purpose of Jesus's person and life.[37] Jesus' initiation, labor, and purpose was wholly oriented toward bringing systemic social change through His inspiring teachings and loving example.

Central to Rauschenbusch's Jesus is the understanding that He "lived in the hope of a great transformation of the national, social, and religious life about him. He shared the substance of that hope with his people, but by his profounder insight and his loftier faith he elevated and transformed the common hope." [38] Accordingly, Rauschenbusch argued that Jesus emphasized the transformation of "single centers of influence and of social nuclei," meaning He envisioned human social progress through transforming social systems.[39] Jesus' scope was universal, emphasizing a "human hope" over

---

[34] Rauschenbusch, *Righteousness and the Kingdom*, 118.
[35] Rauschenbusch, *A Theology for the Social Gospel*, 147.
[36] Rauschenbusch, *Righteousness and the Kingdom*, 118.
[37] Rauschenbusch, *Christianity and the Social Crisis*, 123.
[38] Rauschenbusch, *Christianity and the Social Crisis*, 53.
[39] Rauschenbusch, *Christianity and the Social Crisis*, 53.

against the previous "Jewish hope" of his people; and the future gaze of that hope turned to "faith in present realities and beginnings, and found its task here and now."[40] This hope for here-and-now transformation resulted in a new type of humanity which was the beginnings of a new social organism and social transformation. As he framed it, "The personality which [Jesus] achieved was a new type in humanity...it became the primal cell of a new social organism."[41] Furthermore, Jesus' life created an entirely new epoch in the social evolution of humanity by introducing a new type of living, and consequently new social standards by which humans were called to live.[42] Jesus could create such an epoch and introduce a new type of living because of who He was in His unique relationship with God.

Rauschenbush described this "unique relationship" thusly: "He is the real revelation of God;" "Jesus experienced God in a new way;" "All His mind was set on God and one with Him."[43] We see the influence of Schleiermacher on Rauschenbusch's understanding of Jesus' deity when he describes Jesus as having an "intuition of God" and "consciousness of God," who is "a perfectly religious personality, a spiritual life completely filled by the realization of a God who is love."[44] Furthermore, Rauschenbush approvingly quotes Johann Fichte's description of Jesus, who

---

[40] Rauschenbusch, *Christianity and the Social Crisis*, 53.

[41] Rauschenbusch, *A Theology for the Social Gospel*, 152.

[42] Rauschenbusch, *A Theology for the Social Gospel*, 152.

[43] Rauschenbusch, *A Theology for the Social Gospel*, 152, 155.

[44] Rauschenbusch, *A Theology for the Social Gospel*, 154-155.

wrote that "The consciousness of the absolute unity of the human and the divine life is the profoundest of insights possible to man. Before Jesus it did not exist...Jesus evidently had this insight"[45] Rauschenbusch's belief that Jesus had a unique God-relationship seems to differ from Nicaea's conception, in that it isn't clear that He believed that Jesus Himself is God. Instead, Jesus the man had a profound connection with and consciousness of the "divine life." Jesus possessed the divine (i.e. God) within himself by nature of His words and deeds. Rauschenbush even states that he is not particularly interested in the "metaphysical problems involved in trinitarian and christological doctrines;"[46] He is not interested in how Jesus is God. Instead, Rauschenbush's interest was in how the "divine *life* of Christ" gained control of human society.

Elsewhere, speaking in trinitarian terms, Rauschenbush argued that the *idea* of the glorified Christ and the Holy Spirit are "nearly identical," stating "Christ and the Spirit are not two distinct forces."[47] He seems to suggest no trinitarian distinction at all between Father, Son, Spirit. In fact, Rauschenbusch suggests the Spirit of God that acted upon the early Christians was simply the inspirational words and deeds of Jesus. Speaking about the early Christians who had a sense of being acted upon by the Spirit of God, Rauschenbush wrote, "do they ever conceive of [the Spirit of God] as anything but the Christ whose words they have

---

[45] Rauschenbusch, *A Theology for the Social Gospel*, 152.

[46] Rauschenbusch, *A Theology for the Social Gospel*, 148.

[47] Rauschenbusch, *The Righteousness of the Kingdom* , 148.

heard and whose person they have loved as they have seen him in the gospels? Do they not feel the personal nearness and guidance and love of their Friend and Master?"[48] Instead of the two forces—Christ and Spirit—acting upon the disciples, Rauschenbusch collapsed them into the "twofold influence of the *one force*, the Logos of God."[49]

Note that the "force" of Christ and the Holy Spirit are not personal. Rather, he defined the *Logos of God* impersonally as the enduring influence of His historic appearance in human history (i.e. the life of Jesus) and the perpetual influence of Himself upon humanity (i.e. the influence of Jesus). Like Ritschl, Rauschenbusch seems to hold that Jesus is not the metaphysical but the moral Son of God. He bluntly states that questions about Christ's divinity are not about nature, but *character*: "We shall come closer to the secret of Jesus if we think less of the physical process of conception and more of the *spiritual* process of desire, choice, affirmation, and self-surrender within his own will and personality."[50] He goes on to accuse "theology" of defining Jesus' divinity in terms of *nature* rather than *character*.[51] Instead, Rauschenbusch seems to insist Jesus' divinity does not consist in an ontological fact, but as the universal human ideal of love He lived.

Ultimately, Jesus came to show humanity that their normal human existence—"the ordinary life of selfishness

---

[48] Rauschenbusch, *The Righteousness of the Kingdom*, 148-149.

[49] Rauschenbusch, *The Righteousness of the Kingdom*, 149. (emph. mine)

[50] Rauschenbusch, *A Theology for the Social Gospel*, 150. (emph. mine)

[51] Rauschenbusch, *A Theology for the Social Gospel*, 150.

and hate and anxiety and chafing ambition and covetousness"—was no life at all, and instead humanity "must enter into a new world of love and solidarity and inward contentment."[52] For Rauschenbusch, then, the secret to Jesus was the new life of love He lived and brotherhood He showed that confronted and transcended the normal ways of living out human existence. Over and against this normal life of humanity, "Jesus set love into the center of the spiritual universe, and all life is illuminated from that centre. This is the highest idealistic faith ever conceived, and the greatest addition ever made to the spiritual possessions of mankind."[53] Jesus brought humanity the universal human ideal of love, which he insists solves for our human problem of selfishness. The true nature of the work of Jesus, then, was establishing the Kingdom with His life and the love and service He modeled, rather than saving humanity through His sacrificial death on the cross.

It seems clear that for Rauschenbusch, the power of Christ to solve our human problem came not through His work on the cross or even chiefly in His teachings. Rather the chief power of Christ is His personality, His enduring example.[54] Even where he comments on the social gospel and atonement, Rauschenbusch holds a solidaric interpretation of Jesus' death rather than a vicarious, substitutionary interpretation.[55] In describing the nature and impact of Jesus'

---

[52] Rauschenbusch, *Christianity and the Social Crisis in the 21st Century*, 42.
[53] Rauschenbusch, *A Theology for the Social Gospel*, 154.
[54] Rauschenbusch, *Righteousness and the Kingdom*, 122.
[55] Rauschenbusch, *A Theology for the Social Gospel*, 258.

death on the cross, Rauschenbusch insisted that Jesus bore six so-called "social sins"[56] that have impacted the whole race and everyone in it. The reader should note, however, that by using the term "bore," Rauschenbusch does not mean vicariously as a substitutionary sacrifice. Instead, he argues that Jesus bore them "by direct experience." He goes on to say, "In so far as the personal sins of men have contributed to the existence of these public sins, he came into collision with the totality of evil in mankind. it requires no legal fiction of imputation to explain that 'he was wounded for our transgressions, he was bruised for our iniquities.' Solidarity explains it."[57] Jesus' atoning death on the cross, then, is defined by his direct experience of the forces of the Kingdom of Evil and their impact on His own life, an experience that was an extension of His life.

Rauschenbusch makes clear that "the death of Christ was an integral part of his life."[58] In fact, he argues that theology makes a "fundamental mistake" when it treats the atoning death of Christ as something separate and distinct from the life of Jesus.[59] Instead, Jesus' death was "wholly of one piece

---

[56] These six sins include: 1) religious bigotry, "the most persistent force that pushed Jesus to death;" 2) the combination of bribery and political power, in which Jesus was a threat to the ruling class both politically and monetarily; 3) corruption of justice, where Jesus was a victim of the court; 4) the mob spirit and mob action, which is the "social spirit gone mad" and which Jesus bore by experience; 5) militarism, in which Jesus "fell into the hands of the war system" from the time of His arrest in Gethsemane to His crucifixion at Golgotha; and 6) class contempt, which is the contempt for the lower class by the upper class and which Jesus bore "when he was nailed to the tree." Rauschenbusch, *A Theology for the Social Gospel*, 248-257.

[57] Rauschenbusch, *A Theology for the Social Gospel*, 248.

[58] Rauschenbusch, *A Theology for the Social Gospel*, 260.

[59] Rauschenbusch, *A Theology for the Social Gospel*, 260.

with his life. He gathered all the radiance of his character and purpose in a focus-point of blazing light, and there he died."[60] Notice that Jesus' character and vocation is squarely in view. At the cross Jesus' higher life, the universal human ideal that He modeled to humanity, was clearly and brightly seen; at the cross Jesus' life-purpose and Kingdom vocation culminated in the most visible and truest picture of love and service. Thus, Rauschenbusch argued that the "spiritual and redemptive value of his death" was not in suffering as a substitute but "in the willingness with which he took himself this highest and hardest part of his life-work."[61] Because Jesus' death and life were one continuous tapestry of love and service, the benefit that Jesus' followers receive from His death is identical to what they receive from His life: His "higher impulse" and model of love and service, manifested as the Kingdom of God.

Rauschenbusch maintains the "higher impulse" of Christ was implanted in His followers, and over time it has blossomed so that we are finally comprehending the "real meaning and spirit of Christ," which was His higher social life for humanity, the Kingdom of God.[62] Christ wanted His life to be in His disciples, so that they would find the chief good of their lives in him: "His thoughts became their thoughts. His sympathies and antipathies were theirs."[63] By taking upon themselves the life example of Christ through adopting His

---

[60] Rauschenbusch, *A Theology for the Social Gospel*, 260.

[61] Rauschenbusch, *A Theology for the Social Gospel*, 261.

[62] Rauschenbusch, *Christianity and the Social Crisis*, 115.

[63] Rauschenbusch, *Righteousness and the Kingdom*, 150.

thoughts and ways, the early followers of Jesus found salvation. The same is true for us today. Jesus' life and example, rather than His death and resurrection, are what solve our human problem.

Through humanity generally, Jesus' personality—His life and example—has endured throughout history as a force that is progressively transforming society from what it is to what it ought to be. As Rauschenbush says, "whenever [Jesus'] personality gains influence over a human soul, the result will be that that soul will go forth to live a revolutionary life."[64] Jesus' powerful example has abiding power because "his true character is forever bursting forth and impelling new men to revolutionary effort;" His life continues to inspire people throughout generations to bring social change and live their best life now.[65] Therefore, we can say that the Kingdom, rather than the atoning death of Jesus, is the mode by which humanity is saved. Jesus saves insofar as He brings in the Kingdom. Thus, as with the other liberals, the Kingdom itself is what saves us.

THE SALVATION OF THE KINGDOM

Like Schleiermacher and Ritschl before him, Rauschenbusch sought to help the Church "once more preach the Kingdom of God as the central and all-embracing doctrine,"[66] which he agreed had been neglected for most of the life of the Church. Rauschenbusch believed that the

---

[64] Rauschenbusch, *Righteousness and the Kingdom*, 128-129.

[65] Rauschenbusch, *Righteousness and the Kingdom*, 129.

[66] Rauschenbusch, *Righteousness and the Kingdom*, 130.

grammar of the Kingdom of God should be given a central place, because "without [the doctrine of the Kingdom of God] the idea of redeeming the social order will be but an annex to the orthodox conception of the scheme of salvation."[67] The "scheme of salvation" to which Rauschenbusch refers is the type of personal salvation common to modern evangelicalism. As he argued, the Kingdom of God "is not a matter of saving human atoms, but of saving social organisms. It is not a matter of getting individuals to heaven, but of transforming the life on earth into the harmony of heaven." [68] Instead of an individualized hope, the Kingdom is a social hope "involving the whole social life of man."[69] Like Ritschl, Rauschenbusch's Kingdom grammar is inherently social rather than individual.

Rauschenbusch defines the social-ness of the Kingdom of God in several ways: it is the "true human society, it is a fellowship of justice, equity, and love;"[70] it means "normal and wholesome human relations;" [71] and the Kingdom is "the better humanity."[72] The Kingdom is inherently social and the highest expression of humanity. It is fundamentally defined as the progressive development of humanity from the-way-it-is to the-way-it-ought-to-be. Human progress and social hope sits at the center of Rauschenbusch's Kingdom grammar. He

---

[67] Rauschenbusch, *A Theology for the Social Gospel*, 131.
[68] Rauschenbusch, *Christianity and the Social Crisis*, 54.
[69] Rauschenbusch, *Christianity and the Social Crisis*, 54.
[70] Rauschenbusch, *Christianity and the Social Crisis*, 62.
[71] Rauschenbusch, *Christianity and the Social Crisis*, 62.
[72] Rauschenbusch, *Christianity and the Social Crisis*, 168.

also described the Kingdom as a "historical force" that seeks to save the human social order within history: "The Kingdom of God is not a concept or an ideal merely, but a historical force. It is a vital and organizing energy now at work in humanity. Its capacity to save the social order depends on its pervasive presence within the social organism."[73] From where does this historical saving force come that advances and saves humanity? The history transforming force of the Kingdom comes from the historical person and continuing inspiring "presence" of Jesus Christ.

As Rauschenbusch insists, we needed someone to come along and show us a better existence, to inspire us with a better way of living the universal human ideal. That person was Jesus, and he came to solve our human problem of selfishness and bad human existence by founding the Kingdom and calling disciples to it as a great revolutionary movement "pledged to change the world-as-it-is into the world-as-it-ought-to-be."[74] Here we see Rauschenbusch's continuity with the liberal tradition of Schleiermacher and Ritschl that preceded him: our salvation comes by way of a transformation of human existence (world-as-it-is) into the human ideal (world-as-it-ought-to-be). Note the generational continuity: our human solution is found in the universal human ideal over against the problem of human existence, which, in reality, means our solution is found in ourselves.

He states plainly that human "ethical and religious forces can really do something to check and prevent the

---

[73] Rauschenbusch, *A Theology for the Social Gospel*, 165. (emph. mine)

[74] Rauschenbusch, *Christianity and the Social Crisis*, 123.

transmission of sin along social channels."⁷⁵ Rauschenbusch contrasts this social view of sin with a "biological transmission," where checking and preventing the transmission of sin is "beyond our control."⁷⁶ This Pelagian understanding of our human solution makes sense because Rauschenbusch has a Pelagian view of human nature. According to him, we on our own have the power to stem the tide of sin; human social forces can prevent social sin. Humans have the capacity within themselves to advance or retard humanity. Consequently, out of our own gumption and ingenuity we humans can and should build the Kingdom to solve our social crises, because such human progress actually "depends largely on us."⁷⁷ We have the power to change the world if we would only use it: we have "the power to win stubborn hearts, the power to uncover social lies, the power to make injustice blush and skulk away, the power to shame immodesty into hiding places."⁷⁸ Curiously, Rauschenbusch neglected the role of the Holy Spirit, relegating the power of human transformation in the force of Jesus' moral example and human gumption and ingenuity. Where he did talk about the Holy Spirit, Rauschenbusch spoke of Him merely as a "religious doctrine" and "energetic religious consciousness."⁷⁹ In omitting the Holy Spirit, humanity is all that's left to work toward bringing about the

---

[75] Rauschenbusch, *A Theology for the Social Gospel*, 68.

[76] Rauschenbusch, *A Theology for the Social Gospel*, 68.

[77] Rauschenbusch, *Righteousness and the Kingdom*, 107.

[78] Rauschenbusch, *Righteousness and the Kingdom*, 108.

[79] See Rauschenbusch, *A Theology for the Social Gospel*, 188-196.

REIMAGINING THE KINGDOM

life transformation that results in social change. Instead of the Holy Spirit, the Kingdom's presence on earth depends upon humanity. We have the power to create social change because we have the power of Jesus' enduring example, which inspires us to live as we ought by living and loving as He did.

In the words of Rauschenbusch, "His life is what counted," a life that was wholly purposed on establishing the Kingdom of God, which is the "historical current of salvation" that extends from Him through history to save humanity.[80] Jesus saves because His inspiring life-example lives on in the Kingdom, which was His revolutionary movement to progress the human social order. Jesus was able to catalyze social change because He alone "fully married the real and the ideal, the life here and the life beyond, the inward perfection and its steady reconstruction of the outward perfection."[81] Because Jesus' life successfully combined real human existence with the essence of the human ideal, He brought the force of the Kingdom to bear on human social order, resulting in universal social salvation.

Rauschenbusch believed that the Kingdom embraces all realms of society, not just the Church; the Church isn't the only place the Kingdom is present. This position is consistent with Ritschl who himself broke from Schleiermacher's conflation of the Kingdom with the Church. Rauschenbusch argued, "The Kingdom of God is not confined within the limits of the Church and its activities. It embraces the whole of human life...The Kingdom of God is in all these [social

---

[80] Rauschenbusch, *A Theology for the Social Gospel*, 165. (emph. mine)

[81] Rauschenbusch, *Righteousness and the Kingdom*, 130.

institutions] and realizes itself through them all."[82] Whether the family, industry, or State, the Kingdom of God is working to transform these social orders, Christian or not. He goes on to say that "Every approximation to [the Kingdom of God] is worthwhile. Every step toward personal purity and peace...carries its own exceeding great reward."[83] It seems that for Rauschenbusch, every human activity that aligns itself with the defining characteristics of the Kingdom counts as Kingdom activity. Every single life can join in with advancing human progress by simply accepting the Kingdom as their own task: "Every human life is so placed that it can share with God in the creation of the Kingdom, or can resist and retard its progress. The Kingdom is for each of us the supreme task and the supreme gift of God." He goes on to say that if we accept the Kingdom task, then we receive the gift of the Kingdom, which is "the joy and peace of the Kingdom as our divine fatherland and habitation."[84] Again, Rauschenbusch seems to suggest that everyone experiences the gift of God's solution to our human problem by doing Kingdom acts.

There is a decidedly universal ring to Rauschenbusch's work, as he envisioned that the Kingdom extended to all of humanity. He suggested that it was guaranteed that "Christ would limit his work not by the bounds of nationality but by the bounds of humanity."[85] Thus, every step forward, "every increase in mercy, every obedience to justice, every added

---

[82] Rauschenbusch, *A Theology for the Social Gospel*, 145.

[83] Rauschenbusch, *Christianity and the Social Crisis*, 338. (emph. mine)

[84] Rauschenbusch, *A Theology for the Social Gospel*, 141.

[85] Rauschenbusch, *Righteousness and the Kingdom*, 83.

brightness of truth would be an extension of the reign of God in humanity, an incoming of the Kingdom of God."[86] Again, Rauschenbusch seems to suggest that every act counts as Kingdom activity, whether the person knows it or not. Rauschenbusch uses several examples to illustrate how the whole life, abilities, and interests of every person can be enlisted as Kingdom work: the life of the farmer who toils for the daily bread of humanity; the engineer who builds bridges over chasms and holds back "the seething river from the cottages of his brother" with dams; carpenters, masons and plumbers who build safe, dry, sunny houses "in which little children will not be strangled to death by poison germs;" even just lawyers and merciful doctors are included in his Kingdom Hall of Fame.[87] Each of these people illustrate how the Kingdom of God embraces every simple, useful everyday act of humanity. And everyone "who fulfills the conditions of the Kingdom" are promised the salvation of Christ.[88] What are those conditions, what defines the "usefulness" of a particular activity? As with Schleiermacher and Ritschl, Rauschenbusch says useful Kingdom activity is loving activity. As long as we love we do Kingdom work; love is the Kingdom-condition.

Rauschenbusch argued that "the Kingdom of God implies a progressive reign of love in human affairs;"[89] it is the

---

[86] Rauschenbusch, *Righteousness and the Kingdom*, 88.

[87] Rauschenbusch, *Righteousness and the Kingdom*, 112.

[88] Rauschenbusch, *Righteousness and the Kingdom*, 97.

[89] Rauschenbusch, *A Theology for the Social Gospel*, 142.

"fellowship of humanity acting under the impulse of love."[90] Because Jesus Christ Himself made love the defining characteristic of God and highest law of human activity, "the reign of God would be the reign of love."[91] And the highest expression of love is "the free surrender of what is truly our own, life, property, and rights."[92] Love is by nature self-sacrifice and the Kingdom of God is a "cooperative labor" in which we actively love others by serving their needs with our abilities.[93] Self-sacrificing service and love is at the center of the Kingdom of God because it was the way of Jesus Himself. As Rauschenbusch writes, "Jesus desired to found a society resting on love, service, and equity." He goes on to say that "when Jesus prepared men for the nobler social order of the kingdom of God, he tried to energize the faculty and habits of love and to stimulate the dormant faculty of devotion to the common good."[94] In the end this new love-defined society is exactly what defines Rauschenbusch's Kingdom grammar. And this love-acting fellowship frames his solution: The Kingdom is what saves us.

CONCLUSION

Put plainly, Rauschenbusch insisted that "a man is saved according as he enters or does not enter the Kingdom."[95] The

---

[90] Rauschenbusch, *A Theology for the Social Gospel*, 155.
[91] Rauschenbusch, *A Theology for the Social Gospel*, 54.
[92] Rauschenbusch, *A Theology for the Social Gospel*, 143.
[93] Rauschenbusch, *A Theology for the Social Gospel*, 55.
[94] Rauschenbusch, *Christianity and the Social Crisis*, 57, 56.
[95] Rauschenbusch, *Righteousness and the Kingdom*, 99.

REIMAGINING THE KINGDOM

dividing lines that once existed between Jew and Greek are now along those who "open their heart to the new life" of the Kingdom and "those who are closed to it."[96] Thus, salvation is found by entering into the universal human ideal initiated by Jesus through His teachings and inspiring example of love, which all people can participate in by nature of their Kingdom-oriented activity. It will help to quote Rauschenbusch to provide a final examination of his Kingdom grammar:

> The fundamental contribution of *every man* is the *change of his own personality*. We must repent of the *sins of existing society*, cast off the spell of the lies of protecting our social wrongs, *have faith in a higher social order*, and *realize in ourselves a new type of Christian manhood* which seeks to overcome the evil in the present world, not by withdrawing from the world, but by revolutionizing it.[97]

There are several items to note in this quotation which aptly summarizes Rauschenbusch's theological positions regarding the Kingdom of God as the solution to the human problem

Notice that Rauschenbush has "every man" in view, which is seemingly consistent with a universalistic view of Kingdom-participation; everyone is (or has the potential to be) Kingdom-oriented, because every action of love counts as Kingdom activity. Furthermore, the problem for which "every man" must solve is the "sins of existing society" and "social wrongs." And every person has the inner capacity to "change" themselves and "realize" a new type of human

---

[96] Rauschenbusch, *Christianity and the Social Crisis*, 51.

[97] Rauschenbusch, *Christianity and the Social Crisis*, 331.

Rauschenbusch's Grammar

existence. They apparently don't need the Holy Spirit to awaken their faith and transform their lives. Instead, individuals themselves are charged with the task of solving their own problem, which comes by "having faith in a higher social order," the universal human ideal or the Kingdom of God. Rather than calling on people to have faith in the finished work of Jesus Christ on the cross and His bodily resurrection, Rauschenbush instead calls people to have faith in *the new way of living*, the higher way of Kingdom living. Ultimately, the object in which we are to place our faith isn't in Jesus Christ, but in the Kingdom of God, which is the consistent liberal appeal for people to have faith in their own self-potential by nature of humanity's potential. Such an appeal was strengthened and renewed one generation later with the *Kingdom* grammar of Paul Tillich.

REIMAGINING THE KINGDOM

CHAPTER 5
Tillich's Grammar

Both Grenz and Olson maintain that Paul Tillich's contribution to 20th-century theology "is comparable to Barth's in terms of overall influence and impact," giving him the title "apostle to the intellectuals."[1] In fact, Tillich graced the cover of TIME magazine on March 16, 1959, where he was recognized for the significance of his theological and philosophical achievements. Already while Tillich was still alive, some argued that his *Systematic Theology* "could go down in history alongside the systems of Aquinas and Hegel...it will stand in the history of philosophical-theologies as one of the distinct systems and another bold attempt to wed the two sciences."[2] Furthermore, the staying power and lasting impact of Tillich has shown itself recently in apparent

---

[1] Grenz and Olson, *Twentieth-Century Theology*, 114.

[2] R. Allan Killen, *The Ontological Theology of Paul Tillich* (Kampen, J. H. Kok, 1956.), 9.

appropriations of his material.³ Thus, it is appropriate to examine this theological heavyweight's understanding of the Kingdom of God in order to trace the generational theological development of *Kingdom* grammar from liberalism to evangelicalism. Tillich's unique contribution to the liberal development of *Kingdom* grammar lay in his emphasis on the historical nature of the Kingdom, insisting that the Kingdom of God is the symbolic expression of both the immanent and transcendent sides of history, functioning as the answer to the problem of the meaning of human history. For Tillich, the Kingdom of God is both in and above history.

TILLICH'S HISTORICAL CONTEXT

Tillich was a German Lutheran who studied at several major universities, including Halle and Berlin, while pursuing a career in ministry. World War I interrupted his theological and ministerial pursuits where he served as a chaplain to the German Army, an experience that profoundly changed him. As Grenz and Olson explain, "His encounters with mass death and destruction became a turning point in his personal life and faith. He suffered two nervous breakdowns and underwent a severe crisis of faith and doubt that transformed his view of God."⁴ It took the war to make Tillich aware of

---

³ In his newest book, *Love Wins: A Book About Heaven, Hell, and the Fate of Every Person Who Ever Lived* (New York: HarperOne, 2011), Rob Bell seems to appropriate several of Tillich's existential theological concepts—including God, the person of Jesus the Christ, Cross, Resurrection, and the Afterlife—in order to argue for a universal salvation.

⁴ Grenz and Olson, *Twentieth-Century Theology*, 115.

the real social conditions of Germany, particularly the conditions of the lower classes and the antagonism that existed between the Bourgeois and labor masses.[5] This social and theological transformation was solidified in his post-WWII experience in America. It was then that he joined many neo-liberals in their sober recognition of the tragic dimensions of human existence and history, a recognition that was lacking in eras before both World Wars. These historical experiences would help give rise to Tillich's theological method and system when combined with a potent philosophical one: existentialism.

In part, the re-emergence of existentialism represents a response to the irrational events of the two World Wars that form part of our historical context. The historic optimism birthed out of the Enlightenment and Industrial Revolution gave way to a realism not felt for generations. In the wake of such human tragedies as war, poverty, and urban stresses, theologians gravitated toward existentialism in order to provide a theological response to tragic twentieth-century existence. Grenz and Olson comment that Tillich "provides perhaps the most lucid example of a neo-liberal who chose existentialism as theology's conversation partner."[6]

Several characteristics of existentialism provide the backdrop to Tillich's own theology and *Kingdom* grammar: existentialism emphasizes the situation into which a person has been thrown, one's "being-in-the-world;" anxiety qualifies man's existence because he realizes that he is not at home in

---

[5] Killen, *The Ontological Theology of Paul Tillich*, 32.

[6] Grenz and Olson, *Twentieth-Century Theology*, 114.

the world and the world is without meaning; such anxiety gives way to authentic living in order to break from ordinary everyday existence; everyday we are confronted with the alienness and meaninglessness of the world, giving us a sickening feeling of danger and insecurity; such confrontations force us to face our fragility and alienness in the world; ultimately, our existence ends in death, the fact of which should cause us to give our lives a significance and purpose in the here and now before we are robbed of the gift of life.[7]

Tillich himself admits to standing within the existentialist movement, correlating the structure of his theology with man's existential questions and concerns. As Livingston writes, "the existentialist stance dominates Tillich's theological method and system."[8] Tillich was strongly impacted by two particular existentialists: Kierkegaard and Heidegger. In fact, Tillich's *The Courage to Be* is his existentialist attempt to solve for Kierkegaard's problems of anxiety, guilt, and despair with an ontology of Being and Non-Being.[9] And while Tillich initially found it hard to accept existentialism, it slowly took root in his mind largely as the result of Heidegger's influence.[10] Some even go so far as to say that had it not been for Heidegger's *Being in Time*, Tillich's ontology would not have developed as it did.[11]

---

[7] Livingston, *Modern Christian Thought*, 348-350.

[8] Livingston, *Modern Christian Thought*, 356.

[9] Killen, *The Ontological Theology of Paul Tillich*, 52.

[10] Killen, *The Ontological Theology of Paul Tillich*, 35, 52.

[11] Wilhelm and Marion Pauck, *Paul Tillich: His Life and Thought* (New York: Harper & Row Publishers, 1989), 98.

Likewise, Andrew O'Neill refers to Tillich's own self-proclaimed passion for "post-Idealist existential responses to Neo-Kantianism evident in Kierkegaard and Heidegger."[12] Particularly, existentialism dominates Tillich's *Kingdom* grammar, affecting his definitions of sin, Jesus' person and work, the Kingdom itself, and even God.

THE PROBLEM FOR WHICH THE KINGDOM SOLVES

As with three generations of liberals before him, understanding how Tillich defined our human problem is vital to understanding how he defined the Kingdom. Tillich's treatment of our human problem is different than how the Church has understood it in the past, but consistent with the view of Schleiermacher, Ritschl, and Rauschenbusch. As Killen argues, "He bases his view of sin upon a consideration of the conditions which he finds existence rather than upon the view of sin given in the Bible."[13] It is important to note at the outset that Tillich's view of sin and the human condition is predicated upon his view of God. What Tillich means by *God* has great bearing on our discussion of Tillich's *Kingdom* grammar, as it plays into his understanding of the problem for which the Kingdom solves. The vague term *Ground of Being* is how Tillich describes our sense of God, doing so in the context of estrangement.

---

[12] Andrew O'Neill, *Tillich: A Guide for the Perplexed* (London: T & T Clark, 2008), 29.

[13] Allan, *The Ontological Theology of Paul Tillich*, 185.

In one sense, we are estranged from the "Ground of our being" because we are estranged from "the origin and aim of our life," estranged from the point of existence.[14] Elsewhere, Tillich indicates this terms stands for God himself: "The name of this infinite and inexhaustible depth and ground of all being is *God*. That depth is what the word *God* means."[15] Tillich does not seem to assume the existence of an actual Being alongside and above others in the traditional sense. Instead, God is understood as *being-itself* or as the *ground of being*. Consistently, Tillich refers to God as an *idea*, an existential idea in which God is the foundation of existence and meaning. "God" is the word that signifies that which is meaningful and gives meaning to existence. As Tillich says, "The word 'God' points to ultimate reality."[16] Note that God is merely a symbol for that which is ultimately meaningful in existence, which means we are merely estranged from the *symbol* rather than the *being* of God.

Rather than believing humanity is separated from an ontological *Being* called God, the Father almighty, maker of all things visible and invisible in the vein of Nicaea, Tillich suggested we are separated from the *aim of our life* and *center of all meaning*. As Tillich argued, "if [God] has no meaning for you, translate it, and speak of the depth of your life, of the source of your being, of your ultimate concern, of what you

---

[14] Paul Tillich, *The Shaking of the Foundations* (New York: Charles Scribner's Sons, 1948), 155.

[15] Tillich, *Shaking of the Foundations*, 57.

[16] Tillich, *Systematic Theology*, 2:94.

take seriously."[17] For Tillich, that which gives meaning to and is of ultimate concern in life, actually *is* God. We are separated and estranged from that which is meaningful in life that which is of ultimate existential concern, which leads to anxiety, despair, and death.[18] Because Tillich believed God was a symbol for that which is of ultimate meaning, Tillich views the human problem as *separation* and *estrangement* from that meaning, which leads to the conditions of meaninglessness, anxiety, and death. As Tillich said, our problem is one of historical existence: "Man's historical existence is threatened,"[19] threatened by each of these conditions. Therefore, our solution must do something with our historical existence by solving our estrangement from the universal ideal.

Tillich's early definition of sin in *The Shaking of the Foundations* provides a glimpse into the formation of his doctrine of sin: "Have the men of our time still a feeling of the meaning of sin? Do they, and do we, still realize that sin does not mean an immoral act, that 'sin' should never be used in the plural, and that not our sins, but rather our sin is the great, all-pervading problem of our life?"[20] Early on, Tillich rejected the notion that sin is an act or a collection of acts, instead interpreting it as a *condition*, a *state* of man's existence. As we will see, this view is not the same as the historic

---

[17] Tillich, *Shaking of the Foundations*, 57.

[18] Tillich, *Shaking of the Foundations*, 97.

[19] Tillich, "Victory in Defeat: The Meaning of History in Light of Christian Prophetism," Interpretation 6 (1952): 18.

[20] Tillich, *Shaking of the Foundations*, 154.

Christian view of original sin. As Tillich argued, there is no "bondage of the will," no original, hereditary sin.[21] Tillich clarified his position by reinterpreting sin entirely: "I should like to suggest another word to you, not as a substitute for the word 'sin,' but as a useful clue in the interpretation of the word 'sin': 'separation'...*sin is separation*. To be in the state of sin is to be in the state of separation."[22] For Tillich, *separation* is key to understanding the human problem. Humanity is separated from that which is of ultimate meaning and the aim of life, which creates the existential conditions of anxiety, meaninglessness, despair, and death. A decade later, Tillich revised and extended this definition to mean *estrangement:* our basic human condition is a "state of estrangement of man and his world from God;"[23] "estrangement points to the basic characteristic of man's predicament."[24]

Tillich did not believe that an original state of Edenic perfection existed. Instead, an original perfection of humanity is rooted in what Tillich called our "state of essential being" and a state of so-called "dreaming innocence,"[25] both symbols and a *state of mind* that signify the way humanity ought to be in created goodness in their essential nature. Accordingly, the traditional notion of "the Fall" is merely a symbol for our "transition from essential to

---

[21] Tillich, *Systematic Theology*, 2:39-41.

[22] Tillich, *Shaking of the Foundations,* 154. (Italc. his); *Systematic Theology*, 2:46.

[23] Tillich, *Systematic Theology*, 2:27.

[24] Tillich, *Systematic Theology*, 2:39, 44, 45.

[25] Tillich, *Systematic Theology*, 2:33.

existential being."²⁶ This transition (i.e. Fall) from essentiality—the ideal of how man *ought to be* in his goodness—to existential estrangement—the reality of *how man is* in his meaningless condition and separation from the aim of life—is simply part of human development and growth.²⁷ In other words, while humanity is innately good, throughout humanity's evolutionary development they have always been estranged from ethical actions that pave the way for that which is of ultimate meaning in life. Thus, man has never been or acted the way he ought. For this reason, like Schleiermacher, Ritschl, and Rauschenbusch before him, Tillich reinterpreted original sin, viewing it not in hereditary terms but in existential terms. As Tillich argued, "The transition from essence to existence is not an *event* in time and space but the transhistorical *quality* of all events in time and space."²⁸ The importance of the idea of the Fall is not that it *happened*, but that it *happens*. Adam is merely a symbol for essential man—how he ought to be, what is the ideal—and symbolizes the transition from essence to existence; original sin is simply the "universal destiny of estrangement" that plagues all people.²⁹ Thus, Tillich insisted that original sin is much more a universal fact and state than a nature out of which individuals act; in their own existence, individuals actualize the universal state of human existence.³⁰ Because we

---

[26] Tillich, *Systematic Theology*, 2:30.

[27] Tillich, *Systematic Theology*, 2:33.

[28] Tillich, *Systematic Theology*, 2:40. (emph. mine)

[29] Tillich, *Systematic Theology*, 2:56.

[30] Tillich, *Systematic Theology*, 2:56.

are separated from the ultimate meaning of existence (i.e. God), we experience a number of negative "consequences" that wreak havoc on our self-existence.

In his existential condition, man is in a state of despair, the pain of which stems from the conflict between what he potentially is (essence) and what he actually is (existence), resulting in self-estrangement.[31] The consequences of this self-estrangement is the loss of meaning and a despairing existence, which ultimately results in death: "Estranged from the ultimate power of being, man is determined by his finitude. He is given over to his natural fate. He came from nothing, and he returns to nothing. He is under the dominion of death and is driven by the anxiety of having to die."[32] Though sin is not the cause of death, it is its sting; self-estrangement from that which is of ultimate meaning is the pain of death, which is much more symbolic than literal: "Death has become powerful—that is to say that the End, the finite, and the limitations and decay of our being have become visible..."[33] According to Tillich, we are not separated from our Creator through collective and personal rebellion, but separated from that which is of ultimate meaning in life, resulting in meaningless, fearful, tragic, miserable existence, culminating in death. Our solution, therefore, must be one that conquers our self-estrangement and brings in love, which Tillich explained is stronger than the conditions of

---

[31] Tillich, *Systematic Theology*, 2:75.

[32] Tillich, *Systematic Theology*, 2:66.

[33] Tillich, *New Being*, 170, 171.

existence.³⁴ For that, we needed a bearer of a solution of love and new existence who shared in our existential condition, yet triumphed over it. We found such a bearer in the existence of Jesus, who brought us the Kingdom by showing us a new, better existence, one we can participate in by following His teachings and deeds.

THE BEARER OF THE KINGDOM: THE PERSON AND WORK OF JESUS

Central to any *Kingdom* grammar is how it defines the person and work of Jesus. There is a consistent pattern among liberal theologians in their definition of Jesus that subsequently shifts their *Kingdom* grammar. Tillich views the historical conceptions of the nature of Jesus (as the) Christ as wholly inadequate to understanding the person of Jesus.³⁵ Whereas the historic Christian faith frames Christology as two natures (i.e. God and human), Tillich argued, "The assertion that Jesus as the Christ is the personal unity of a divine and human nature must be replaced by the assertion that in Jesus as the Christ the eternal unity of God and man has become a historical reality."³⁶ Instead, Jesus is "divine" because the essence of the universal human ideal (i.e. God) became a historical reality in His life. Consistent with the

---

³⁴ Tillich, *New Being*, 172.

³⁵ As he says, ""The doctrine of the two natures in the Christ raises the right questions but uses wrong conceptual tools. The basic inadequacy lies in the term 'nature.' When applied to man, it is ambiguous; when applied to God, it is wrong. This explains the inescapable definitive failure of the councils, e.g. of Nicaea and Chalcedon."; Tillich, *Systematic Theology*, 2:142.

³⁶ Tillich, *Systematic Theology*, 2:148.

other liberal theologians, Jesus is the moral Son of God, not the metaphysical one.

In describing Jesus' divinity, Tillich used language similar to Schleiermacher, Ritschl and Rauschenbusch to emphasize His loving life and character. Some typical examples include: "In the picture of Jesus...is the picture of a man in whom God was manifest in a unique way;"[37] "They look at a life which never lost the communication with the divine ground of all life, and they look at a life which never lost the union of love with all beings;"[38] Jesus is "one man in whom God was present without limit...;"[39] "In the face of Jesus the Christ, God 'makes his face shine upon us."[40] Tillich goes on to say that the Gospels give us a picture of Jesus' existence that never broke with the universal human ideal, despite His participation in "the ambiguities of human life;" through His words, deeds, and sufferings we see the expression of this universal human ideal.[41] Thus for Tillich, the words and deeds, the teachings and life of Jesus equate Him with the divine. Jesus is divine because He maintained a unity with the essence of ultimate meaning, which in the end cashes out as

---

[37] Tillich, *Systematic Theology*, 2:146.

[38] Tillich, *New Being*, 74.

[39] Tillich, *New Being*, 178-179.

[40] Tillich, *New Being*, 100.

[41] Tillich, *Systematic Theology*, 1:135-136.

love (i.e. God).⁴² In Jesus, ultimate existence is present because "God" is present and unveiled in the picture of Jesus; the universal human ideal of loving activity was present in Jesus' existence. In His existence we find the essence of our salvation, the New Being, which is the Kingdom of God.

In *The New Being*, Tillich defines the central message of Christianity as the message of a new existence, the New Being that appeared with Jesus who brought a new state of things.⁴³ The New Being is contrasted with the old being, the old state of things under existential estrangement, and finds its historical expression in the symbol *Kingdom of God*. The New Being—a term synonymous with the Kingdom of God—is a reality "in which the self-estrangement of our existence is overcome, a reality of reconciliation and reunion, of creativity, meaning, and hope."⁴⁴ Tillich makes plain that Jesus the man, as the Christ, is the bearer of this new way of existing, of the Kingdom of God. Jesus' existence and life on earth made Him the Christ, the bearer of the New Being, because He possessed the characteristics and qualities of the one who has overcome estrangement and separation from that which is of ultimate meaning in life, mainly love. ⁴⁵ As

---

⁴² In *The New Being*, 26, Tillich seems to suggest God and love are not two realities but one, where the statement "God is love" is taken to mean God is equated with love, rather than *characterized* by it. As Tillich later wrote, "It is a rare gift to meet a human being in whom love—and *this means God*—is so overwhelmingly manifest...For God is love. And in every moment of genuine love we are dwelling in God and God in us;" Tillich, *New Being*, 29. For Tillich, God is an experience of that which is ultimately meaningful and essential to good existence, which is love. In other words, God actually *is* Love.

⁴³ Tillich, *New Being*, 15.

⁴⁴ Tillich, *Systematic Theology*, 1:49.

⁴⁵ Tillich, *Systematic Theology*, 2:121.

with Schleiermacher, Ritschl, and Rauschenbusch before him, Tillich believed our solution is found in Jesus' *life*, not His death, though Tillich did believe the cross mattered.

For Tillich, the "Cross of Christ" was an extension of His life and is where Jesus' "subjection to existence is expressed."[46] Tillich was not so much concerned with a single event in history in which Jesus was nailed to and hung from a cross. For him, the *story* of the cross of Jesus is what counts: "The story of the Cross of Jesus as the Christ does not report an isolated event in his life, but that event toward which the story of his life is directed and in which the others receive their meaning."[47] The cross, then, merely symbolizes the whole of Christ's cruciform life, the meaning of which is that He subjected himself to the ultimate negativities of existence, which He did not allow to separate Him from that which is of ultimate meaning in life.[48] Tillich insisted it was through the negation at the cross by the old existence that the new reality of the Kingdom was born here and now, which is what ultimately "saves" humanity. The New Being is the new reality that enables personal conquest over separation from ultimate meaning because of our existence. It is a saving "power" that triumphs over existence. The saving work of Jesus, then, is to be conceived of as the healing and saving power of the New Being right now in history that came through Jesus' life and culminated in His death.[49] The New

---

[46] Tillich, *Systematic Theology*, 2:153.

[47] Tillich, *Systematic Theology*, 2:158.

[48] Tillich, *Systematic Theology*, 2:158.

[49] Tillich, *Systematic Theology*, 2:167.

Tillich's Grammar

Being is central to Tillich's *Kingdom* grammar, providing the solution to our human problem, which is found wherever essence overcomes existence, wherever love is actualized in existence through human progress.

Though Jesus is considered the bearer of the New Being because He brought the Kingdom, Tillich seems to suggest He isn't necessarily the exclusive saving power of the New Being: "he is the ultimate *criterion* of every healing and saving power...in him the healing quality is complete and unlimited. Therefore *wherever* there is saving power in mankind, it must be judged by the saving power of Jesus as the Christ."[50] In other words, while Jesus is the *standard* for salvation—in that He bore and represented the new reality of existential conquest with the Kingdom in His life and death—He is not the exclusive entry point into it. Instead, He stands as a model for *anything* that brings hope, healing, reconciliation, and love. Where there is healing, there is the New Being and the Kingdom in history; where there is love, there is the Kingdom of God. Love powerfully solves our problem, because it creates what Tillich calls the *unambiguous life*, the new existence of the Kingdom. Tillich often frames our human problem—existential estrangement—using the term *ambiguity*. Ambiguity is the gap between the essential and the existential, between the intended created goodness and estrangement from that goodness. The quest for the New Being, then, is a "quest for the unambiguous life...All creatures long for an unambiguous fulfillment of their

---

[50] Tillich, *Systematic Theology*, 2:168. (emph. mine)

essential possibilities."[51] In other words, humans want to reconcile *how they are* with *how they ought to be*, to reconcile reality with ideality. The unambiguous life is rooted in the reality of the Kingdom, the true nature of Jesus' work that provides the answer to meaningless historical existence. Tillich envisioned the personal and historic saving effects of the manifestation of the New Being of the Kingdom threefold: participation, acceptance, and transformation. These three characteristics reflect the classical theological categories for Jesus' saving work: Regeneration, Justification, and Sanctification.

First, Tillich emphasized that "the saving power of the New Being in Jesus as the Christ is dependent on man's participation in it."[52] Jesus brought the new eon of the Kingdom and individuals are called to enter that new reality, participating in it and being reborn in that participation.[53] For Tillich, participation in the New Being comes through faith, which he defined as *"the courage to say yes to one's own life* and life in general, in spite of the driving forces of fate, in spite of the insecurities of daily existence, in spite of the catastrophes of existence and the breakdown of meaning;"[54] it is the *"reception of the message that one is accepted."*[55] Acceptance of one's acceptance, then, is the entry-point into the new reality of the Kingdom and solution to our problem

---

[51] Tillich, *Systematic Theology*, 3:107.

[52] Tillich, *Systematic Theology*, 2:176.

[53] Tillich, *Systematic Theology*, 2:177.

[54] Tillich, *New Being*, 53. (emph. mine)

[55] Tillich, *Systematic Theology*, 3:130; 2:85. (emph. mine)

of meaningless, anxious existence. After this self-acceptance through regeneration comes the central event of salvation: Justification. For Tillich, Justification is the act of "making man that which he essentially is from which he is estranged," which he argues is in no way dependent on man himself, but instead is God's acceptance of humanity despite themselves.[56] In reality, however, the reconciliation of which justification provides is not to a being *God*. Instead, we are reconciled to *existence* because we cease to be hostile toward ourselves, a hostility that manifests itself in self-rejection, disgust, and self-hatred.[57] Ultimately, then, we are called to be reconciled to *ourselves* in our existential condition. Tillich says this very thing when he remarkably equates reconciliation to God with reconciliation to ourselves.[58]

That Tillich framed reconciliation as self-centered rather than God-centered makes sense considering he believes the questions of the past—How do I become liberated from the Law? (Paul); How do I find a merciful God? (Luther)—are replaced by a new one: How do I find meaning in a meaningless world?[59] Finding myself, making sense of my life, and exploring self-meaning leads to salvation. According to Tillich, a person is justified "because they are accepted with respect to the ultimate meaning of their lives."[60] Is this not simply double-speak for a person accepting the meaning of

---

[56] Tillich, *Systematic Theology*, 2:178.

[57] Tillich, *New Being*, 21.

[58] Tillich, *New Being*, 21.

[59] Tillich, *Systematic Theology*, 3:227.

[60] Tillich, *Systematic Theology*, 3:228.

their own lives, or perhaps accepting how they ought to live (i.e. their essentiality) as a way of creating meaning for themselves in their meaningless existence? Tillich himself said that a person experiences this mark of the Kingdom when "one accepts one's self as something which is eternally important, eternally loved, eternally accepted. The disgust at one's self, the hatred of one's self has disappeared."[61] Deep reconciliation to and acceptance of one's own self-existence, then, is the heart of Tillich's *Kingdom* grammar. Reconciliation to God was not Tillich's concern; he was concerned with self-reconciliation to one's self-existence.

Finally, after participating in the New Being of the Kingdom and accepting that they are accepted, humanity experiences salvation as transformation by the New Being of the Kingdom. Tillich defined this transformation as, "the process in which the power of the New Being transforms personality and community, inside and outside the church."[62] Sanctification is the progressive conquest of the ambiguities of the personal life, a closing of the gap between essential goodness and existential estrangement, between how man ought to be and how he is, between ideality and reality.[63] Tillich conceived this process of transformation as a completely human endeavor. Humanity has the power within itself—by consequence of Jesus' participation and overcoming of existential estrangement and his example of love by living the universal human ideal—to close the gap and

---

[61] Tillich, *New Being*, 22.

[62] Tillich, *Systematic Theology*, 2:179-180.

[63] Tillich, *Systematic Theology*, 2:180.

make the transition from essence to existence, from *life-as-it-is* to *life-as-it-ought-to-be*.

While the effects of Jesus' saving Kingdom-work are historical in scope, it is clear they apply to individuals universally, too. As Tillich stated, "Only if salvation is understood as the healing and saving power through the New Being in all history is the problem put on another level. In some degree *all men participate* in the healing power of the New Being.[64]" As he wrote elsewhere, "No longer is the universe subject to the law of death out of birth. It is subject to a higher law, to the law of life out of death by the death of him who represented eternal life." In His suffering and death Jesus as the Christ represented the height of ultimate meaning, which means that "nature has received another meaning; history is transformed and you and I are no more what we were."[65] *All individuals* right now participate in the inner/trans-historical reality of the New Being found in the symbol of the Kingdom of God, because the ultimate solution to our human problem is the Kingdom; the *Kingdom* is what saves us.

THE SALVATION OF THE KINGDOM

For Tillich, the Kingdom of God "is the answer to the ambiguities of man's historical existence, but because of the multidimensional unity of life, the symbol includes the answer to the ambiguity under the historical dimension in all realms of life...[It] embraces the destiny of the life of the

---

[64] Tillich, *Systematic Theology*, 2:167. (emph. mine)
[65] Tillich, *New Being*, 178-179.

REIMAGINING THE KINGDOM

universe..." In the symbol *Kingdom of God*, historical existence is conquered in an ultimate transformation and fulfillment of history.[66] The Kingdom of God stands as the historical symbol for the ultimate meaning and aim of all life universal through the appearance of the new eon. This new eon is the reunion of *essence* and *existence* experienced within human life and history.[67] Jesus of Nazareth as the Christ was the one who brought in the new eon and with it the end of history. As Tillich argued, "In Jesus as the Christ the kingdom of God is present...Jesus is the Christ, that is, he who brings the kingdom."[68] With the event of Jesus, the reality of the Kingdom of God appeared in a personal life and created a group with a historical consciousness, the church.[69] This symbol, which was instantiated in the person and life of Jesus and later His church, is the answer to the concrete ways in which the gap between the ideal and real is expressed in humanity's historical existence; it is the means by which we are saved. The symbol includes both "the struggle of unambiguous life with the forces which make for ambiguity, and the ultimate fulfillment toward which history runs."[70] Tillich's *Kingdom* grammar, then, includes both the inner-historical and transhistorical.

---

[66] Tillich, "Victory in Defeat," 23.

[67] The term *existence* is the real, the way things are; *essence* is the universal ideal, the way things ought to be.

[68] Tillich, "Victory in Defeat," 25.

[69] Tillich, "Victory in Defeat," 25. Tillich also equates *existence* with ambiguity and *essence* with unambiguous life.

[70] Tillich, *Systematic Theology*, 3:108.

Tillich's Grammar

Tillich was dissatisfied with the typical, liberal definitions of the Kingdom that centered on progressivistic, utopian, and transcendental interpretations of history.[71] Tillich instead reinterpreted the Kingdom of God as the answer to the questions implied in historical existence, specifically the meaning of history,[72] though his ultimate answer seems as progressivistic and utopian as previous generations. In his own definition, Tillich's unique contribution to liberal *Kingdom* grammar lay in his immanent-transcendent dichotomy: "[The Kingdom of God] has an inner-historical and a transhistorical side. As inner-historical, it participates in the dynamics of history; as transhistorical, it answers the questions in the ambiguities of the dynamics of history."[73] Tillich's *Kingdom* grammar has both a dynamic and static element, an immanent and transcendent element: "It works and struggles in history and it is the eternal fulfillment beyond history...The Kingdom of God is fighting in history and victorious above history."[74] Tillich insisted that in order for the symbol *Kingdom of God* to provide a proper answer to the questions concerning the meaning of history, it must be immanent and transcendent at the same time. The terms *Spiritual Presence* and *Eternal Life* both help Tillich's *Kingdom* grammar explain the Kingdom of God's activity in and above history and salvation of humanity.

---

[71] Tillich, *Systematic Theology*, 3:356.

[72] Paul Tillich, "Victory in Defeat: Meaning of History in Light of Christian Prophetism," *Interpretation* 6 (1952): 23.

[73] Tillich, *Systematic Theology*, 3:357.

[74] Tillich, "Victory in Defeat," 24.

REIMAGINING THE KINGDOM

The first side of the Kingdom of God is what Tillich called the *Spiritual Presence*. It is the inner-historical, immanent aspect of his *Kingdom* grammar. Tillich said the Spiritual Presence is "the presence of the Divine Life within creaturely life;"[75] it manifests itself in all history and "acts upon [Mankind] in every moment...there is always New Being in history;"[76] and the Spiritual Presence is a "meaning-bearing power which grasps the human spirit in an ecstatic experience."[77] This symbol stands as the power that brings meaning to bear upon the experience of an individual at the point the human mind is grasped by that which is of ultimate meaning.[78] Furthermore, the Spiritual Presence is the guide of what Tillich termed *essentialization*, the inner-historical process of regaining one's essence: "the Spiritual Presence elevates the human spirit into the transcendent union of unambiguous life and gives the immediate certainty of reunion with God."[79] In tangible form, the Spiritual Presence embodies itself in the so-called *Spiritual Community*, created by the New Being under the conditions of finite existence,[80] which is really any group that embodies the universal human

---

[75] Tillich, *Systematic Theology*, 3:107.

[76] Tillich, *Systematic Theology*, 3:140.

[77] Tillich, *Systematic Theology*, 3:115. *Ecstasy* is the "state of being grasped by the Spiritual Presence," or the human spirit under the conditions of existence being under the control of the universal human ideal. Ibid, 3:114.

[78] Tillich, *Systematic Theology*, 1:111-12, describes ecstasy in this way: "Ecstasy ('standing outside one's self') points to a state of mind which is extraordinary in the sense that the mine transcends its ordinary situation...Ecstasy occurs only if the mind is grasped by the mystery, namely, by the ground of being and meaning."

[79] Tillich, *Systematic Theology*, 3:128.

[80] Tillich, *Systematic Theology*, 3:150.

ideal of love. Spiritual Community isn't identical with Christian churches, but is a catch-all word for all who give themselves over to the Kingdom of God, the universal human ideal.

The second aspect of the Kingdom of God and symbol for the unambiguous life above history is *Eternal Life*. It is the transcendent side of the resolution to the problem of ambiguity, symbolizing the fulfillment of history and the "permanently present end of history."[81] In this fulfillment, Tillich argued that somehow the positive elements of history —which are taken as positive human progress, especially ethical—live on while the negative parts of humanity are removed.[82] He argued that which has been created will not be lost—including all humans—only the elements of existence that are contrary to the essence of life will be removed. This end, however, is actually not really an end at all. Instead, Tillich envisioned it as present; the future end is present now.

Tillich re-interpreted *eternal* to mean *right now*, hence his well-known phrase the *eternal now*. He argued that the past and future meet in the present, that both are included in the "now." Accordingly, "the eschaton becomes a matter of present experience without losing its futuristic dimension: we

---

[81] Tillich, *Systematic Theology*, 3:396.

[82] Tillich, *Systematic Theology*, 3:397. As Tillich writes, "nothing which has been created in history is lost, but it is liberated from the negative elements with which it is entangled within existence. The positive becomes manifest as unambiguously positive and the negative becomes manifest as unambiguously negative in the elevation of history to eternity. Eternal Life, then, includes the positive content of history, liberated from its negative distortions and fulfilled in its potentialities."

stand *now* in the face of the eternal, but we do so looking ahead toward the end of history and the end of all that is temporal in the eternal."[83] What is clear is that there is no terminus to history, in the classical Christian sense; history is not fulfilled but rather history continues to unfold and is elevated to the eternal—that which is of ultimate meaning in existence. What happens now, then, is a progressive "burning" of that which is negative in favor of that which is positive, which is symbolized by the idea of ultimate judgment. Tillich argued that *judgment* means "here and now, in the permanent transition of the temporal to the eternal, the negative is defeated in its claim to be positive, a claim it supports by using the positive and mixing ambiguously with it."[84] Notice that people are not in view here, but non-entities called "the positive" and "the negative," which might include the negative outcomes of human progress like pollution and ethical actions like war. While both terms are incredibly vague, they must be synonyms for the *essential* and *existential* that Tillich argues throughout his works. In other words, *Eternal Life*—the transhistorical side of the Kingdom of God—is the *telos*, the aim of human development; it is that which is essentially positive in place of the existentially negative. This aspect of the Kingdom is a present experience of future ends, a transition from essence to existence right here and now in which humanity is saved through right-now human progress.

---

[83] Tillich, *Systematic Theology*, 3:396.

[84] Tillich, *Systematic Theology*, 3:397.

Tillich's Grammar

As with Schleiermacher, Ritschl, and Rauschenbusch before him, human progress right now is central to Tillich's *Kingdom* grammar and human salvation. Tillich wrote, "The hope of the Kingdom of God is not the expectation of a perfect stage at the end of history...The hope of mankind lies in the here and now, whenever the eternal appears in time and history," whenever the universal human ideal shows up in human existence.[85] In many ways, the Kingdom is an ongoing activity that "is happening always in history, the fight of the divine and the demonic, the defeat and the ultimate victory of the kingdom of God"[86] in our human existence in which we recover our essence from existence in history. The Kingdom and the salvation it brings is manifested historically whenever there is human progress and development, including pre-Christianity with Israel's exodus from Egypt, "the East-West encounter in present-day Japan," and development of Western culture in the last 500 years.[87] Tillich's *Kingdom* grammar is the historical progressive gap-closing process between essence and existence, which seems to cash-out as humanistic progress. Ending racism, curing cancer, and building the United Nations—all good things for sure—are modern day marks of human progress, marks of the unambiguous life in history and expressions of the Kingdom of God. Fundamental to this human progress and unambiguous life is love.

---

[85] Paul Tillich, "The Right to Hope," *The Christian Century* 107 no 33 (1990): 1066.

[86] Tillich, "Victory in Defeat," 26.

[87] Tillich, *Systematic Theology*, 3:365.

Tillich insisted that the Kingdom progressively unfolds through acts of love, a consistent element of the Kingdom grammar that has developed from Schleiermacher thus far: "The Kingdom of God does not come in one dramatic event sometime in the future. It is coming here and now in every act of love...."[88] Tillich states plainly that "the Kingdom of God is the universal actualization of love."[89] Furthermore, he states that the communal expression of the Kingdom—the Spiritual Community—is fundamentally a community of love.[90] Likewise the church, one form of the Spiritual Community that embodies the Kingdom, is fundamentally a community of love.[91] Love is fundamental to the Kingdom because, as Tillich argued, faith and love cannot be separated because faith is the "state of being grasped by the Spiritual Presence," by the inner-historical side of the Kingdom, which is the universal human ideal of love.[92] Thus, love is central to one's religious experience and communal expression of that experience, because when one exercises faith one exercises love. Because the Kingdom comes here and now in every act of love, Tillich's Kingdom grammar has the familiar ring of universalism.

Tillich makes it clear that anything that brings meaning to history counts as Kingdom activity. Using the Greek word *kairos* to describe the in-breaking event of the central

---

[88] Tillich, "The Right to Hope," 1066. (emph. mine)

[89] Tillich, *Systematic Theology*, 3:413.

[90] Tillich, *Systematic Theology*, 3:156.

[91] Tillich, *Systematic Theology*, 3:177, 178.

[92] Tillich, *Systematic Theology*, 3:177.

Tillich's Grammar

manifestation of the Kingdom, Tillich argued that this appearance "is again and again re-experienced through relative '*kairoi*' in which the Kingdom of God manifests itself in a particular breakthrough,"[93] suggesting the Kingdom manifests itself universally in various ways. As he says, the "Kingdom of God and the Spiritual Presence are never absent in any moment of time…The Kingdom of God is always present…" reinforcing the universal symbol *Kingdom*.[94] Furthermore, his use of the terms *Spiritual Community* and *the churches* suggests a universalism. As Tillich explains, "The predicate of intensive universality keeps the churches wide open—*as wide as life universal*. Nothing that is created and essentially good is excluded from the life of the churches and their members." He goes on to say "There is nothing in nature, nothing in man, and nothing in history which does not have a place in the Spiritual Community and, therefore, in the churches of which the Spiritual Community is the dynamic essence."[95] *The churches* do not seem to correlate with The Church,[96] but instead function as a catch-all for any "spiritual presence" that helps progress historical existence toward the universal human ideal and fights against the forces that impede this transition from existence to essence.[97] There are Christian varieties that stand as the "manifest church," but also "latent churches" that seem to have no connection with

---

[93] Tillich, *Systematic Theology*, 3:370.
[94] Tillich, *Systematic Theology*, 3:317, 372.
[95] Tillich, *Systematic Theology*, 3:170. (emph. mine)
[96] In *Systematic Theology*, 3:377.
[97] Tillich, *Systematic Theology*, 3:375.

REIMAGINING THE KINGDOM

Christianity, yet have always manifested the Kingdom in embodied form [i.e. Spiritual Community] throughout history.[98] Everyone, then, can solve our problem by advancing humanity through acts of love. In the end everyone wins because love wins through the saving power of the Kingdom.

CONCLUSION

Like Schleiermacher, Ritschl, and Rauschenbusch before him, Tillich defined the Kingdom of God as a progressive unfolding of the universal human ideal within historical existence that ultimately saves humanity. Though his own *Kingdom* grammar was shaped by Existentialism, it was still consistent with three prior generations of Protestant liberal grammar. Humans are affected by their miserable, meaningless existence, which causes them to actualize the universal state of sin in their own existence. They are not the problem; their environment and existence is. The solution to that problem of bad existence must do something to help reconstruct a meaningful existence. That meaningful existence came with the person of Jesus, who successfully conquered human existence by living the universal human ideal. He didn't just found the Kingdom, as other liberals have suggested; He *was* the Kingdom by nature of His loving life, which climaxed in His death.

As with three liberal generations, the Kingdom is the mode by which humanity is saved, rather than the work of Jesus on the cross. Jesus saves insofar as He brings in the Kingdom, rather than through His atoning death. Thus, the

---

[98] Tillich, *Systematic Theology*, 3:376.

Tillich's Grammar

Kingdom itself is what saves us, and all of humanity can and will benefit from this saving power. Humanity as a whole, in light of the historic actualization of the universal human ideal in the life of Jesus in human existence, can conquer their own estrangement from the universal human ideal. What all people must do is accept that they are already accepted. A person must simply accept that he already has all that he needs to live his best meaning-filled life right now, in this life.

REIMAGINING THE KINGDOM

CHAPTER 6
McLaren's Grammar

Thus far, we have traced the generational development of Protestant liberal *Kingdom* grammar. McLaren's grammar includes several of their features. He teaches that sin is social and environmental, rather than an inherited sinful nature and guilt; Jesus is the moral, rather than metaphysical, Son of God; in founding the Kingdom of God, it was necessary that Jesus lived but he gives no compelling reason that Jesus' death was necessary; the Kingdom of God is concerned with humanity's progress; the Kingdom comes into the here-and-now through the power of loving human action; it is inclusive, in that every act counts as Kingdom acts; it is universalistic, in that everyone will be saved; the Kingdom centers on the words, deeds, and suffering of Jesus—His inspiring personality provides humanity the proper example of the universal human ideal; and ultimately, the Kingdom is concerned with bringing the universal human ideal to bear on human existence, empowering individuals and society to reach their fullest potential and live their best life right now.

Our purpose in tracing the development of Protestant liberal kingdom grammar is to show how a progressive form of contemporary evangelicalism is the twenty-first century expression of that grammar. Here, we turn toward the task of proving the original thesis of this examination: the *Kingdom* grammar of the Emergent Church movement is continuous with four previous generations of Protestant liberalism, including how it defines the Kingdom of God, who is in, how one gets in, and how it solves for our human problem. From Schleiermacher through Ritschl, Rauschenbusch, and Tillich, one can trace the general themes of Protestant liberalism to the Emerging Church movement, particularly to one of its most well-known articulators, Brian McLaren. While he might eschew the "liberal" label,[1] he has obviously perpetuated Protestant liberal *Kingdom* grammar. And though some may say no single voice speaks for the Emergent Church movement,[2] it is clear he is one of the most significant theological voices in the movement, someone who is referred to as the "grandfather" of the Emergent Church. Therefore, it is appropriate to examine his *Kingdom* grammar in order to understand how the generational development of liberal *Kingdom* grammar is impacting contemporary Evangelicalism.

---

[1] See McLaren, *A Generous Orthodoxy*, 131-143.

[2] Tony Jones, *The New Christians: Dispatches from the Emergent Frontier* (San Francisco: Jossey-Bass, 2008), 231. The reference is included in Appendix B: "A Response to Our Critics," from 2005.

McLaren's Grammar

MCLAREN'S HISTORICAL CONTEXT

In 2001 Brian McLaren, a little known pastor just north of Washington D.C., began influencing street-level theological conversations within evangelicalism with his landmark book, *A New Kind of Christian*.[3] Through the book's two protagonists—Pastor Dan and Neo—McLaren took the reader on a redefining journey through evangelical's core theological doctrines. God, creation, sin, Christ, the cross, resurrection, and judgment were all addressed and countered with alternative possibilities that formed the foundation for the Emerging Church conversation. It was also a reflection of his own spiritual journey, one that began with fundamentalism via the Plymouth Brethren and culminated in "a quest for honesty, for authenticity, and for a faith that made more sense to me and to others...learning that there is a kind of faith that runs deeper than mere beliefs."[4] Many in our post-9/11, recession-racked, socially-upended world who entered this church conversation found resonance with McLaren's own spiritual quest.

Those seeking to do Christianity on the other side of modernity have found solace in the questions and alternative answers offered by McLaren in response to what many perceive to be stogy, stuffy, stale theology that has outlived its lifecycle. In place of a theology he claims is beholden to modernity, McLaren insists "we need a new way of believing,

---

[3] McLaren has since retired from pastoring *Cedar Ridge Community Church* and been named one of the "25 Most Influential Evangelicals In America," *Time Magazine*, February 7, 2005.

[4] McLaren, *A New Kind of Christianity*, 6, 8.

not simply new answers to the same old questions, but a new set of questions. We are acknowledging that the Christianities we have created deserve to be reexamined and deconstructed...so that our religious traditions can be seen for what they are...they are evolving, embodied, situated versions of the faith."5 Like other Emergents, McLaren has set out to construct a new, fresh, alternative Christianity in light of postmodernity, because he like others realized "something isn't working in the way we're doing Christianity any more."6

Of postmodernism, McLaren writes, "I see the postmodern conversation as a profoundly moral project in intension at least, a kind of corporate repentance among European intellectuals in the decades after the Holocaust."7 In embracing the *generous orthodoxy* descriptor of Hans Frei, McLaren embraces a post-foundationalism posture characteristic of postmodernism to describe his flavor of Christianity.8 Postmodernism as an intellectual movement surfaced in the late 1960s as a surrogate to the post-structuralism of France, which itself was rooted in Kantian philosophy.9 As Carl Raschke explains, "Postmodernism in this sense was nothing more or less than a theory of language that served to demystify previous theories of language

---

5 McLaren, *A New Kind of Christianity*, 18, 27.

6 McLaren, *A New Kind of Christianity*, 9.

7 Brian McLaren, "Church Emerging: Or Why I Still Use the Word *Postmodern* but with Mixed Feelings," in *An Emergent Manifesto of Hope* (Ed. Doug Pagitt and Tony Jones; Grand Rapids: BakerBooks, 2007, 144.

8 See McLaren, *A Generous Orthodoxy*.

9 Carl Raschke, *The Next Reformation: Why Evangelicals Must Embrace Postmodernity* (Grand Rapids: Baker Academic, 2004), 35, 37.

routinely utilized to undercut the language of belief,"[10] particularly the "language of belief" rooted in modernity. Stanley Grenz notes, "postmodernism signifies the quest to move beyond modernism. Specifically, it involves a rejection of the modern-mindset, but launched under the conditions of modernity."[11] Grenz goes on to describe how the modern mind is defined by the Enlightenment project, which exalted the individual rational man to the center of the universe. The goal of the human intellectual quest was "to unlock the secrets of the universe in order to master nature for human benefit and create a better world," an ethos that particularly characterized the twentieth century through technology.[12] Postmodernism, on the other hand, says there can be no objective, autonomous knower because knowledge is not mechanistic and dualistic, but historical, relational, communal, and personal; reality is relative, indeterminate, intuited and participatory.[13] Three names are almost routinely associated with the postmodern project: Jacque Derrida, Jean François Lyotard, and Michael Foucault.

Derrida is considered the father of French deconstruction, a method for rethinking long held beliefs and intellectual assumptions. One of his primary contributions to postmodern philosophy was his often repeated phrase: "there is nothing outside the text." Here, Derrida champions the

---

[10] Raschke, *The Next Reformation,* 37.

[11] Stanley Grenz, *A Primer on Postmodernism* (Grand Rapids: Eerdmans Publishing, 1996), 2.

[12] Stanley Grenz, *A Primer on Postmodernism,* 3.

[13] Stanley Grenz, *A Primer on Postmodernism,* 7-8.

postmodern sentiment that interpretation is an inescapable part of being human and experiencing the world; life is interpretation all the way down because we all bring something to the table out of our cultural, economic, and religious context. For postmoderns, no realm of pure reading exists beyond the realm of interpretation. Lyotard is known for his "incredulity toward metanarratives," which isn't so much a rejection of grand stories, but the manner in which those stories legitimize themselves. In other words, it is not the stories themselves that are the problem, but the way they are told (and to a degree why they are told). As James K. A. Smith argues, "For Lyotard, metanarratives are a distinctly modern phenomenon: they are stories that not only tell a grand story, but claim to be able to legitimate or prove the story's claim by an appeal to universal reason."[14] Smith continues, "What characterizes the postmodern condition, then, is not a rejection of grand stories in terms of scope or in the sense of epic claims, but rather an unveiling that all knowledge is rooted in some narrative or myth. The result, however, is what Lyotard describes as a 'problem of legitimation' since what we thought were universal criteria have been unveiled as just one game among many."[15] All claims to universal truth are reduced to one story among many stories. These stories are conditioned by their own sets of cultural and historical rules, a point McLaren and other Emergent Christians are quick to point out. Finally, Foucault,

---

[14] James K. A. Smith, *Who's Afraid of Postmodernism* (Grand Rapids: Baker Academic, 2006), 65.
[15] Smith, *Who's Afraid of Postmodernism*, 69.

McLaren's Grammar

the master institutional de-constructor was famous for his often quoted phrase, "power is knowledge." Foucault led the charge in cultivating a "deep hermeneutic of suspicion" that marks our postmodern culture's relationship to Institutions of Power, including and especially the institution of the Church. Like Nietzsche, Foucault traced the lineage of secret biases and powerful prejudices that lay submerged beneath institutional truth claims, especially those ideas deemed "moral" or "normal" by institutions like Christianity. According to Foucault, nothing that is "true" is innocently and purely discovered. Instead, what those institutions (State and Religious) deem normal and moral are covertly motivated by various interests of power. It is out of this historical milieu that McLaren's Kingdom grammar has been constructed.

THE PROBLEM FOR WHICH THE KINGDOM SOLVES

Like four generations preceding him, McLaren defines the problem at the root of his *Kingdom* grammar differently than the historic Christian faith's conception of the problem defined by original sin. Through his protagonist Neo in his *New Kind of Christian* trilogy, McLaren contends the Christian story has been distorted, because early Christianity imported "the Greek idea of a fall from a perfect, unchanging, ideal, complete, harmonious, fully formed world into a world of change, challenge, conflict..."[16] McLaren

---

[16] McLaren, *The Story We Find Ourselves In*, 52. This is later affirmed and further developed in *A New Kind of Christianity*, 33-45.

rejects original sin; he insists there is no event of "the Fall" or corresponding "original sin" and "total depravity" in which humanity plunged into rebellion and alienation, resulting in an inherited sinful nature.[17] Instead, the framing narrative of humanity is one of systemic progression and ascent, with corresponding descent resulting in "new depths of moral evil and social injustice."[18] Accordingly, human nature has not "fallen" but is still fundamentally good,[19] progressing from an embryonic stage to a higher stage of existence. As one can see, McLaren's understanding of human nature reflects Rauschenbusch's own strong appropriation of evolutionary doctrine. As the Earth's story is one of emergence, so too is humanity's; our story is not a fall from perfection into a state of imperfection, but "unfolds as a kind of compassionate...classic coming-of-age story."[20] McLaren does not see just one single cataclysmic crisis but "an avalanche of crises."[21] As humans "come of age" they grow beyond God,

---

[17] McLaren, *A New Kind of Christianity*, 43. In an endnote McLaren asserts that these terms "frequently derive their meaning from a story that is, I believe, inherently un-Jewish and unbiblical, and so when they are read into the biblical story, they distort and pollute it." 266n.15.

[18] McLaren, *A New Kind of Christianity*, 51.

[19] McLaren, *Story We Find Ourselves*, 52: As McLaren says, "the God-given goodness in creation isn't lost...God's creative fingerprint or signature is still there, always and forever. The evil of humanity doesn't eradicate the goodness of God's creation, even though it puts all of that goodness at risk."

[20] McLaren, *A New Kind of Christianity*, 49, 51.

[21] McLaren, *The Story We Find Ourselves*, 53-54, 56. He writes, "all involve human beings gaining levels of intellectual and technological development that surpass their moral development—people becoming too smart, too powerful for their own good...Human beings leave their identity, their life, their story as creatures in God's creation...As they become more independent, they lose their connection to God, their sense of dependence...So they experience alienation from God."

and their relationship deteriorates in progressive, fitful "experiences of alienation." McLaren equates sin with "stagnation and decay," saying, "Because of this counter-emergent virus we call sin, the stages, episodes, and levels do not always unfold as they should. There are setbacks, stagnations, false starts, premature births, retardations, impatient rebellions, emergence defects, and failed attempts at emergence."[22] Sin is anti-progress, it is the opposite of the type of human progress (i.e. emergence) the Kingdom of God promotes, and for which we will see solves our human problem. What impedes human progress are bad systems and stories.

In his re-imagined framing narrative, individuals are no longer the issue, but human systems: Rather than individuals acting out of their sinful nature and sinning, "socioeconomic and technological advances" lead to moral evil and social injustice.[23] In the words of McLaren, "it's a story about the downside of 'progress'—a story of human foolishness...the human turn toward rebellion...the human intention toward evil."[24] The problem is not that humans rebelled against God and are rebels or that humans did evil and are evil. For McLaren, the story is one where humans collectively create evil, damaging and savaging God's good world; it is a story where "humans have evil intent" instead of being evil themselves. Those evil intentions are not the result of an evil nature, but the bad systems and stories that consume

---

[22] McLaren, *A Generous Orthodoxy*, 282.

[23] McLaren, *A New Kind of Christianity*, 51.

[24] McLaren, *A New Kind of Christianity*, 54.

humanity. McLaren believes the main dysfunctions of humanity are existential; he frames the crisis of the human condition as an existential crisis of prosperity, equity, and security.[25] These three crises form the "cogs" in what McLaren terms the *suicide machine*.[26] The suicide machine is a metaphor for "the *systems* that drive our civilization toward un-health and un-peace."[27] McLaren envisions the driving force behind our broken, problematic condition to reside in the systems of the world rather than in the individual person. According to him, humanity suffers from a "dysfunction of our societal machinery," which is operated not by single individuals but by humanity acting together."[28] In other words, individual sinful human nature is not the problem, but rather a universal sin of society, which of course is how four generations of liberals defined the human problem: Rauschenbusch said sin was social, Schleiermacher and Ritschl said our problem was a kingdom or systemic "web" of sin and evil.

In *A New Kind of Christianity*, McLaren illustrates this explanation of the human condition and reality of so-called "social sin." Using the story of the Israelites in Exodus, he explains that it is a story of "liberation from the external oppression of social sin," while also celebrating "liberation from the internal spiritual oppression of personal sin."[29]

---

[25] McLaren, *Everything Must Change*, 5.

[26] McLaren, *Everything Must Change*, 53.

[27] McLaren, *Everything Must Change*, 53. (emphasis mine)

[28] McLaren, *Everything Must Change*, 65.

[29] McLaren, *A New Kind of Christianity*, 58.

McLaren's Grammar

Because McLaren does not believe that sin is part of human nature because of an event of rebellion, he must mean something different by "internal spiritual oppression of personal sin." It seems even this internal oppression is related to the social systems of sin, because he asserts that the Israelites were freed from "the *dominating powers* of fear, greed, impatience, ingratitude, and so on."[30] The power of Fear and Ingratitude were the oppressors, which in this Exodus narrative apparently resulted from years of being "debased by generations of slavery."[31] This slave framing story, then, is what contributed to the Israelites communal and individual commitment to "fear, greed, impatience, ingratitude, and so on." The internal compulsion toward greed, for example, was an internal power that resulted from the external system of slavery and the bad framing narrative out of which Israel was liberated. Thus, our ultimate problem is bad systems and stories.

Unlike the traditional historic faith that locates the problem of the human condition in individual sinfulness and an inherited sinful nature, McLaren believes humans are in trouble because we are in bondage to the "dominant societal machinery," which entices us to keep faith in its systems of wealth, security, pleasure, and injustice.[32] This faith and bondage has led to a sort of universal consciousness that is driven by destructive, dysfunctional framing stories. The global crises of which McLaren says we must be saved are the

---

[30] McLaren, *A New Kind of Christianity*, 58. (emphasis mine.)

[31] McLaren, *A New Kind of Christianity*, 58.

[32] McLaren, *Everything Must Change*, 271.

symptoms and consequences of the dysfunction, resulting in a collection of human evil. Dysfunctional societal machinery, destructive framing narratives, and collective human evil are our problems. Rather than sinning out of an inner, natural compulsion, innately good humans are compelled to act badly because of these environmental forces; bad systems and bad stories cause us to misbehave. Thus, we need a better system and a better story to solve for our human problem. We find both in the alternative system and story of the Kingdom which came through the person and life-work of Jesus of Nazareth.

THE BEARER OF THE KINGDOM: THE PERSON AND WORK OF JESUS

At the heart of liberal *Kingdom* grammar is the person of Jesus of Nazareth, whose chief work was founding the historical movement of the Kingdom of God through His loving life example. The same is true for McLaren: the man Jesus is important because of His revolutionary Kingdom movement and model of loving life. While the historic Christian faith recognizes Jesus Christ as God and in some way a penal substitutionary sacrifice for the sins of the world, McLaren recognizes neither. Instead, Jesus is merely the best teacher of a better way of living, the one who lived the best way to be human, and one who is our best picture of the character of God. In *The Story We Find Ourselves In*, McLaren describes Jesus as a "revolutionary" who was a "master of living."[33] According to McLaren, "Jesus really is in

---

[33] McLaren, *The Story We Find Ourselves In*, 115, 121, 122.

McLaren's Grammar

some mysterious and in a unique way sent from God and full of God."[34] Notice McLaren does not say Jesus *is* God, but merely a messenger of sorts from God. His fellowship with God comes from His ethical way of living; Jesus is Divine because He *acts* divinely. As with four generations of liberals before him, McLaren seems to view Jesus as the moral not the metaphysical Son of God.

McLaren affirms this characterization in his most recent book, *A New Kind of Christianity*, by insisting that Jesus "brings us to a new evolutionary level in our understanding of God...the experience of God in Jesus requires a brand-new definition or understanding of God," because He "gives us the highest, deepest, and most mature view of the character of the living God."[35] McLaren's emphasis on the "character of God" finds substantial resonance with four generations of liberalism: "When you see [Jesus], you are getting the best view afforded to humans of the character of God;" "Jesus serves as the Word-made-flesh revelation of the character of God;" and "the invisible God has been made visible in his life. 'If you want to know what God is like,' Jesus says, 'look at me, my life, my ways, my deeds, my character.'"[36] Elsewhere he writes that Jesus simply identifies Himself *with* God, telling His disciples that those who had seen Him had in "some real way" also seen God.[37] In a "mysterious and unique way" Jesus is full of God. He shows, images and expresses God's

---

[34] McLaren, *The Story We Find Ourselves*, 122.

[35] McLaren, *A New Kind of Christianity*, 114, 115.

[36] McLaren, *A New Kind of Christianity*, 118, 128, 222.

[37] McLaren, *The Secret Message of Jesus*, 31.

character. This view of the person of Jesus is liberal in general and starkly Ritschlian in particular.

From McLaren's earliest writings one can detect his theological trajectory and emphasis of Jesus as "teacher" and "liver." In explaining Jesus as "Lord," McLaren argues this means Jesus "was the master of living...it would mean that no one else could take the raw materials of life...and elicit from them a beautiful song of truth and goodness. [The disciples] believed Jesus' way was higher and more brilliant, and the right way to launch a revolution of God."[38] Elsewhere he writes that Jesus' message and teachings is an "alternative framing story" that can "save the system from suicide," a message that focuses "on personal, social, and global transformation in this life."[39] Furthermore, "Jesus' life and message centered on the articulation and demonstration of a radically different framing story—one that critiques and exposes the imperial narratives as dangerous to itself and others."[40] The best teacher, way, and picture of God is the perfect solution to McLaren's problem, because as we already saw we need a better example to follow in order to live differently and avert dysfunction and destruction. Jesus' mastery over life through His higher, more brilliant way of living and alternative message provides the existential solution to our existential problem. Fundamentally, the solution Jesus provides through His work is the Kingdom of

---

[38] McLaren, *The Story We Find Ourselves In*, 121.

[39] McLaren, *Everything Must Change*, 73, 22.

[40] McLaren, *Everything Must Change*, 154-155.

McLaren's Grammar

God, which is exactly how liberal *Kingdom* grammar has framed the solution for four generations.

Central to the work of Jesus is His vocation as the founder of the Kingdom of God, the one in whom the original way of human existence was found, taught and modeled to the world. McLaren insists that Jesus did not come to start a new religion, but to announce a new kingdom, a new way of life;[41] He was the founder of a new countermovement to all other human regimes.[42] Through His life and teachings, Jesus "inserted into human history a seed of grace, truth, and hope that can never be defeated," a seed that will "prevail over the evil and injustice of humanity and lead to the world's ongoing transformation into the world God dreams of."[43] Because the human problem is bad systems and stories, we need a new system and a new story to repair and heal us. Jesus provides humanity the solution through his teachings on the Kingdom of God and example of living out the way of that Kingdom. McLaren makes it clear that the central point of Jesus is the Kingdom of God: "[Jesus] came to launch a new Genesis, to lead a new Exodus, and to announce, embody, and inaugurate a new kingdom as the Prince of Peace. Seen in this light, Jesus and his message has everything to do with poverty, slavery, and a 'social agenda.'"[44] He insists that Jesus himself "saw these dynamics at work in his day and proposed in word and deed a new

---

[41] McLaren, *A New Kind of Christianity*, 139.

[42] McLaren, *The Secret Message of Jesus*, 66.

[43] McLaren, *Everything Must Change*, 79-80.

[44] McLaren, *A New Kind of Christianity*, 135.

alternative. Jesus' creative and transforming framing story invited people to change the world by disbelieving old framing stories and believing a new one: a story about a loving God who calls all people to live life in a new way."[45] We are called to follow Jesus in this new way by following His teachings and example of love.

McLaren believes our problem is the dysfunctional systems and destructive stories of our world. Therefore, our solution came when God called Jesus as a messenger to show us a better way of living and teach us a better story: the Kingdom system and Kingdom story. McLaren agrees with Schleiermacher, Ritschl, Rauschenbusch and Tillich before him that the work of Jesus is fundamentally rooted in founding and living the Kingdom of God. Furthermore, Jesus is the vehicle of the Divine because of the way He lived and taught. Through His vocation as founder of the Kingdom of God Jesus was filled with God—meaning He acted like God would act on earth—and ultimately revealed the character of God by what He did and with what He said. In so acting and revealing, Jesus is the vehicle for an existential solution to our existential problem. As McLaren rhetorically asks, "Is Jesus' healing and transforming framing story really powerful enough to save the world?"[46] Because McLaren believes our systems and stories are the problem, our solution is found in an alternative system and story, which we find in Jesus' message on the Kingdom of God. McLaren answers his question thusly:

---

[45] McLaren, *Everything Must Change*, 237-274.

[46] McLaren, *Everything Must Change*, 269.

McLaren's Grammar

> if we believe that God graciously offers us a new way, a new truth, and a new life, we can be liberated from the vicious, addictive cycles of our suicidal framing stories. That kind of faith will save us...our failure to believe [Jesus' good news] will keep us from experiencing its saving potential, and so we'll spin on in the vicious cycles of Caesar.[47]

According to McLaren, Jesus' teachings on the Kingdom provides the liberation we need from the systems and stories of the world by providing an alternative new system and story, a new way, truth, and life. We find salvation when we "transfer our trust from the way of Caesar to the way of Christ."[48] Notice that McLaren calls people to transfer their trust to the *way* of Christ rather than *person* of Christ. McLaren urges us to transfer our trust from the world's systems and stories—from our bad *existence*—to the system and story of Christ's Kingdom, because the Kingdom is the actual work of Jesus. As with four generations preceding him, McLaren's *Kingdom* grammar fundamentally insists that human salvation isn't found in a *name* (i.e Jesus Christ), but a *movement*—the Kingdom of God.

THE SALVATION OF THE KINGDOM

In one of his clearest definitions of the Kingdom, McLaren defines the Kingdom of God as "a reality into which we have been emerging through the centuries, which is bigger than whatever we generally mean by 'Christianity' but

---

[47] McLaren, *Everything Must Change*, 270.
[48] McLaren, *Everything Must Change*, 271.

at the same time is what generously orthodox Christianity is truly about."[49] In the same section he equates the Kingdom to "the way of Jesus," which is "the way of love and the way of embrace."[50] The Way of Jesus and Kingdom of God "integrates what has gone before so that something new can emerge."[51] And toward what are we emerging? The universal human ideal, the essence of what it means to human: McLaren writes, "Jesus invitation into the Kingdom of God was an invitation into *the original universe, as it was meant to be*."[52] In this definition are several features consistent with liberal *Kingdom* grammar: the Kingdom is transcendent in that it is equated with an ultimate reality that supersedes any particular religion, representing the universal ideal, the essence of human existence; it is immanent in that it is most closely embodied in humanity in the life and way of Jesus and is concerned with historical transformation; it is progressivistic in that the Kingdom takes humanity from a lower level of living to a higher level of existence; it is fundamentally about love-inspired action; finally, it is universal, in that McLaren's grammar has all of humanity squarely in view.

Like the four generations preceding McLaren, his Kingdom grammar is inherently defined by love-inspired action: he suggests the only way for the Kingdom of God to save humanity is through "weakness and vulnerability,

---

[49] McLaren, *A Generous Orthodoxy*, 288.

[50] McLaren, *A Generous Orthodoxy*, 287.

[51] McLaren, *A Generous Orthodoxy*, 287.

[52] McLaren, *The Secret Message of Jesus*, 53. (emph. mine)

sacrifice and love;"[53] McLaren argues that the central governing "policy" of the Kingdom is universal love;[54] he insists the way of Christ, the way of the Kingdom, is inherently the "way of love;"[55] the mission of the Church itself is defined by the single goal of "forming Christlike people, people who live the way of love, the way of peacemaking, the way of the kingdom of God, the way of Jesus;"[56] and finally, the Kingdom of God advances, gains ground "with reconciling, forgiving love: when people love strangers and enemies..."[57] This love activity flows from Jesus Himself who was the first Master at loving activity, which culminated at the cross. For McLaren, the cross is a stage upon which Christ renders a grand performance illustrating God's love, acceptance, and new Kingdom way of sacrifice and suffering. Jesus' life and message has been one of non-violence and triumph over enemies through peace and self-sacrifice. Like the other liberals, the cross is the culmination of those teachings as an exposé on love. Rather than joining in with the "'shock and awe' display of power as Roman crucifixions were intended to do," McLaren says Jesus gives us a "'reverence and awe' display of God's willingness to accept rejection and mistreatment..."[58] In this display of "Christ crucified," McLaren says "we see that the lowly way of Christ,

---

[53] McLaren, *The Secret Message of Jesus*, 69.

[54] McLaren, *A New Kind of Christianity*, 154.

[55] McLaren, *A New Kind of Christianity*, 168.

[56] McLaren, *A New Kind of Christianity*, 171.

[57] McLaren, *The Secret Message of Jesus*, 69.

[58] McLaren, *A New Kind of Christianity*, 158-159.

the vulnerable way of love, is the only way of life."[59] And this life is Kingdom-life. This love-inspired life is what transforms and saves humanity.

Consistent with the four previous generations of liberals, McLaren's *Kingdom* grammar is inherently progressivistic vis-à-vis humanistic change. As he says, "God stands ahead of us in time, at the end of the journey...and washes over us with a ceaseless flow of new possibilities, new options, new chances...This newness, these possibilities are always 'at hand,' 'among us,' and 'coming' so we can 'enter' the larger reality and transcend the space we currently fill." He goes on to say, "We constantly *emerge from what we were* and are into *what we can become*,"[60] equating the Kingdom of God with emergence, with humanistic progress. McLaren rhetorically asks, "What does the future hold? the answer begins, '*That depends on you and me.* God holds out to us at every moment a brighter future; the issue is whether we are willing to receive it and work with God to create it. We are participating in the creation of what the future will be.'"[61] That the future depends on you and me is patently consistent with Rauschenbusch's *social gospel*. Along with Schleiermacher, Ritschl, and Tillich, McLaren believes that we are the makers of our best life now, we are responsible for bringing into existence the best version of ourselves, the universal human ideal; we are responsible for saving ourselves. This is the case because humanity—individuals and as a community—is the

---

[59] McLaren, *A New Kind of Christianity*, 169.

[60] McLaren, *A Generous Orthodoxy*, 283, 284. (emph. mine)

[61] McLaren, *A New Kind of Christianity*, 196. (emph. mine)

McLaren's Grammar

actual *medium* that contains the Kingdom of God, right here and now.[62] Furthermore, all people are called, through their own power and choice, to live in the radical new way of the Kingdom. As McLaren states, "we do indeed have the choice today and every day to seek it, enter it, receive it, live as citizens of it, invest in it, even sacrifice for it," which, depending on this choice, will create two very different worlds and futures: one hellish and one heavenly.[63] Thus, McLaren urges everyone to "start doing the next good thing now," so that the good of the Kingdom will prevail by love, peace, and endurance of suffering, while bad ethical acts like domination, violence, and torture will be overcome through our collective human effort.[64]

Ultimately, salvation is participation in the Kingdom of God, which McLaren calls participatory eschatology. While McLaren contends conventional eschatologies have cultivated resignation, fear, and aggression, participatory eschatology inspires much more:

> a passion to do good, whatever the suffering, sacrifice, and delay because of a confidence that God will win in the end; courage, because God's Spirit is at work in the world and what God begins God will surely bring to completion; a sense of urgency, because we are protagonists in a story; and humility and kindness, because we are aware of our

---

[62] McLaren, *The Secret Message of Jesus*, 101.

[63] McLaren, *The Secret Message of Jesus*, 181.

[64] McLaren, *Everything Must Change*, 146.

ability to miss the point, lose our way, and play on the wrong side.[65]

Furthermore, McLaren argues that the death and resurrection of Jesus are paradigms for this salvation in which we ourselves are to participate in anticipation of God's coming Kingdom: we join with Jesus in dying (metaphorically to our pride and agendas, literally in martyrdom as a witness to God's Kingdom and justice); we rise again in triumph "through the mysterious but real power of God. In this cruciform way, we participate in the ongoing work of God, and we anticipate its ultimate success."[66] For McLaren, our dying and rising with Christ are symbolic of our rejection of and triumph over the dysfunctional systems and destructive stories of our world; we are called to die to the bad ethics of the world and rise to new life by living like Jesus. Thus, salvation is entirely existential, in that His loving example is what saves us from our bad existence, an existential salvation that extends to the whole human race.

In this definition of humanistic progress, we find the familiar ring of universalism present in liberal *Kingdom* grammar. McLaren believes God's wish and hope is for all of humanity to grow toward Christlikeness, because we are *all* children of God.[67] In fact, McLaren believes that "a person can affiliate with Jesus in the kingdom-of-God dimension without affiliating with him in the religious kingdom of Christianity. In other words, I believe that Christianity is not

---

[65] McLaren, *A New Kind of Christianity*, 200.

[66] McLaren, *A New Kind of Christianity*, 200-201.

[67] McLaren, *A Generous Orthodoxy*, 283.

the kingdom of God. The ultimate reality is the kingdom of God..."[68] Because the Christian faith is not the single container of God's reign, the Kingdom is universal; it is a universal human ideal instantiated in the person and life of Jesus whom all may join simply by emulating Him. McLaren insists that everyone is a potential agent of the Kingdom by nature of people's loving activity, like the taxi cab driver McLaren references who treated his guests with special care and respect; Carter had within him the spirit of the Kingdom of God and was a secret agent of the Kingdom.[69] For McLaren this can be true because the Kingdom is about our daily lives, it is a daily way of life centered around Jesus' loving message and life example. He stresses the Kingdom is about so-called *purposeful inclusion*, because it "seeks to include all who want to participate in and contribute to its purpose,"[70] which of course is humanistic progress toward bringing the universal human ideal—in McLaren's words, the original universe as it was meant to be—to bear on human existence. Consequently, McLaren finds it "fascinating" to think that thousands of Muslims, Buddhists, Hindus, and even former atheists and agnostics could come from the east and west and north and south "to enjoy the feast of the kingdom in ways that those bearing the name Christian have not."[71] McLaren would believe this possible because he believes that anything that contributes to humanistic progress counts as Kingdom

---

[68] McLaren, *A Generous Orthodoxy*, 282n.141.

[69] McLaren, *The Secret Message of Jesus*, 85-89.

[70] McLaren, *The Secret Message of Jesus*, 167.

[71] McLaren, *The Secret Message of Jesus*, 217.

activity; any loving-act that subverts the prevailing systems and stories solves for our human problem and provides individual salvation.

In the end, because we are called to live in the system and story of the Kingdom by living the teachings of Jesus, McLaren says ultimate salvation at judgment will be based on behavior, not beliefs: "God will examine the story of our lives for signs of Christlikeness...These are the parts of a person's life that will be deemed worthy of being saved, remembered, rewarded, and raised to new beginnings."[72] Giving food and water to the needy, showing mercy, welcoming the stranger, and being generous like Jesus is what God cares about, what will result in salvation. Conversely, "all the unloving, unjust, non-Christlike parts of our lives...will be burned away, counted as unworthy, condemned, and forgotten forever."[73] Notice the implicit universalism embedded in McLaren's soteriology: in the end, everyone will find salvation, because, as Tillich taught, the positive will live on while the negative will not. Ultimately, then, our salvation depends upon our *existence*, it depends upon how we live, whether we walked the path of Jesus in word, deed, and suffering. Since "no good deed will be forgotten," we are urged to "start doing the next good thing now and never give up until the dream comes true," until God's Kingdom comes.[74] Therefore, in reality, salvation comes not through *Jesus'* saving act on the cross, but through every *human* act

---

[72] McLaren, *A New Kind of Christianity*, 204.

[73] McLaren, *A New Kind of Christianity*, 204.

[74] McLaren, *Everything Must Change*, 146.

that lives out Jesus' way of life. In many ways, each person is his own savior, because every act of love counts as Kingdom acts, as saving acts that bring the universal ideal to bear on existence. In reality, the *Kingdom* saves us through humanistic progress, rather than through Jesus.

CONCLUSION

This *Kingdom* salvation of which McLaren and Emergent grammar speaks is wholly consistent with four generations of liberal *Kingdom* grammar. In this *grammar*, our human problem is not a sinful nature but dysfunctional systems and destructive stories. Rather than bound by sin on the inside, we are oppressed on the outside by bad social and spiritual systems and stories. Jesus is the antidote, the cure for these bad systems and stories because He provided the alternative system and story of the Kingdom through His life and teachings. For McLaren, the Kingdom of God is "A life that is radically different from the way people are living these days, a life that is full and over flowing, a higher life that is centered in an interactive relationship with God and with Jesus...an extraordinary life to the full centered on a relationship with God."[75] He contends this is what the Apostle John termed "eternal life," or "life of the ages." Through his Kingdom message and Kingdom way of living, "Jesus is promising a life that transcends 'life in the present age'...[he] is offering a life in the new Genesis, the new creation that is 'of the age' not simply part of the current regimes, plots, kingdoms, and

---

[75] McLaren, *The Secret Message of Jesus*, 37.

economies created by humans."[76] Jesus came, then, to liberate us from these old regimes (i.e. dysfunctional systems) and plots (i.e. destructive stories), to teach and show us the highest, best way found in the Kingdom. He came to end *life-as-we-know-it* and usher in *life-as-it-ought-to-be*; Jesus' life saves, rather than His death and resurrection. This essence of what it means to be human is rooted in universal brotherly love. The Kingdom represents this ultimate reality, which comes when anyone does any act of love, whether cleaning a local river, launching an adult literacy program, or returning a dropped set of keys to a stranger on a busy city sidewalk. Somehow these love-inspired acts collectively bring in the future we all long for, burning up the negative in the process and enveloping all of humanity in its arms of inclusion. And in the end, while Jesus' life provides the example and way, humanity is its own savior. That is the obvious, logical conclusion to liberal *Kingdom* grammar, which McLaren recites *in toto*.

---

[76] McLaren, *A New Kind of Christianity*, 130.

CHAPTER 7
Conclusion

This examination has demonstrated that the Emergent Church's *Kingdom* grammar is continuous with four previous generations of Protestant liberal theologians. This grammar teaches that sin is social and environmental, rather than an inherited nature and guilt—their view of sin is Pelagian; Jesus of Nazareth, the person who bore the solution to our problem, is not God, but merely divine by nature of living out the universal human ideal; the work of Jesus is His life, rather than His atoning death—His death is important insofar as it was the climax of his life of love; and the Kingdom of God is the means by which humanity is saved—humanity is beckoned to place their faith in this *way* of Jesus rather than His person and work. In the end, the gospel of the Emergent Church is identical with the good news of liberalism: the Kingdom of God, the universal human ideal and essence of human existence, has come near in the life of Jesus; live your best existence now by turning from the destructive stories and dysfunctional systems of this world and turning toward everyday acts of brotherly love. We conclude this examination by considering an observation and a few implications that contemporary appropriations of liberal Kingdom grammar are already having within evangelicalism.

First, an observation: in tracing the generational development of liberal Kingdom grammar it was interesting to note the ways in which the focus on the Church itself shifted and waned. When Schleiermacher introduced the language of the Kingdom back into the Church's theological discourse, the Church was squarely in view: He equated the Kingdom with the Church. Ritschl maintained such a connection, yet broadened the Kingdom to include those well beyond its borders. By the time Tillich formulated his own theological enterprise, the Church had become a symbol and mostly unnecessary. Likewise, in McLaren's theological missive arguing for a new kind of Christianity, the Church is roundly ignored in favor of the Kingdom as the ultimate religious reality. This gradual downplaying and dismissal of the Church makes sense, as the Church is simply one faith community that embodies the universal human ideal and is important only insofar as it was the original religious organization that perpetuated Jesus' teachings. Now in our postmodern polytheistic context, there is even more pressure to downplay and negate the role of the Church as the particular embodiment of Christ and agent of the Kingdom. Such maneuvers have two implications for the future of mainstream evangelicalism.

Conclusion

First, it was noted at the beginning how the terms *mission*, *evangelism*, and *gospel* seem to have shifted over the past few years in light of the resurgent use of the Kingdom of God. While perhaps the nature of Jesus and His substitutionary work on the cross is not in danger of losing their meaning and significance in such circles, one has to wonder how using the Kingdom in ways liberals have for generations will begin to affect mainstream evangelical commitment to core evangelical convictions, mainly conversionism and activism—particularly evangelistic. Popular Evangelical magazines such as *RELEVANT*, books on Christian cultural engagement such as *AND: The Gathered and Scattered Church*[1] and *For the City: Proclaiming and Living Out the Gospel*,[2] and young church leader conferences like *Catalyst* emphasize doing good by living like Jesus. Not that this emphasis is necessarily a bad thing. It seems, however, that in so emphasizing the Kingdom in ways that liberals have for years—mainly transforming human existence through mundane and supramundane acts of love—mainstream evangelicals are in danger of losing sight of what has always been central to evangelicalism, and authentic, historic Christianity.

Furthermore, evangelicals should think twice about appropriating the grammar of the Kingdom in ways liberals have because of the implications that grammar has for the Christian faith itself. How liberals arrive at their definition of

---

[1] Hugh Halter and Matt Smay, *AND: The Gathered and Scattered Church* (Grand Rapids: Zondervan, 2010).

[2] Darin Patrick and Matt Carter, *For the City: Proclaiming and Living Out the Gospel* (Grand Rapids: Zondervan, 2010).

Kingdom depends on how they define sin, the person and work of Jesus, and other aspects of historic orthodoxy. In light of that grammar, then, what is to say mainstream evangelicals will not join progressives in transforming, say, the meaning of the cross itself? Already some have accused proponents of substitutionary atonement of holding a view akin to "divine child abuse."[3] And while some do not go as far as this language they wonder whether we should speak of the cross in language that side-steps traditional substitutionary language altogether in favor of alternative atonement views, such as *Christus Victor*. What is to stop mainstream evangelicals from eventually downplaying the significance of Jesus' death in favor of Jesus' significant life? Perhaps more importantly, if the deeds and teachings of Jesus are all that matter, then what would stop some evangelicals from fudging on the *person* of Jesus, including His deity? Without sounding apocalyptic, if evangelicals continue to use the language of the Kingdom in ways that liberals have for generations, they risk the potential of joining them in the other beliefs that supplied the context and definition of that grammar. So the first implication in adopting liberal *Kingdom* grammar is the danger of losing sight of the historic Christian faith.

Secondly, the Kingdom grammar of liberals and the Emergent Church has massive implications for the future of missions and evangelism. As the introduction noted, a new generation is thinking differently about the nature of evangelism at home and missions abroad. For instance, in

---

[3] McLaren, *The Story We Find Ourselves*, 102.

Conclusion

times past the typical evangelical college would take students on Spring Break trips to key beaches around the country to share the gospel with Spring Break revelers. While such methods of evangelism could be contested, it is worth noting that now it is more common for such colleges to take trips to serve the homeless in Seattle or build wells in Africa than it is to share the gospel with people in need of a Savior. Missions is now about acts of love in the interest of serving our neighbor, rather than acts of gospel proclamation in the interest of seeing our neighbor saved. Furthermore, alongside a shift in emphasis in missions has been a shift in evangelism, the hallmark of mission work of yore. Rather than evangelism being the proclamation of the gospel, people now define evangelism using the maxim often ascribed to St. Francis of Assisi: preach the gospel at all times, if necessary use words. Words that urge repentance, belief, and confession are considered unnecessary, being abandoned in favor of actions of acceptance, service, and love.

The gospel is now framed as the Kingdom coming to our here-and-now rather than justification by faith in Christ. While the Kingdom is part and parcel of the gospel of Jesus Christ, it is being pronounced at the expense of the justification provided through Jesus' death and resurrection. Such pronouncement not only has implications for the future of mission and evangelism, but the gospel itself. Therefore, it behooves evangelicals to reconsider their *Kingdom* grammar in order to guard their *gospel* grammar. Yes, we must pray for God's Kingdom-rule to break into our existence in increasing measure. But we do so with the realization that it was God

Himself through His Son's life, death, and resurrection that made it possible in the first place. It is not the *Kingdom* that saves us, but Jesus Christ alone.

AFTERWORD

If I have learned anything in this academic exercise it's this: theology matters. Getting the "pieces" of theology right, as much as we can in our finiteness, matters because when we get one of those pieces "wrong," the rest fall in lockstep.

How one defines our human problem has great bearing on how one defines our human solution. How one defines our human solution has great bearing on how one defines the One who bore that solution. This book has demonstrated as much in its overview of the generational development of Protestant liberal theology. When you define our human problem environmentally, then our solution must do something with our environment; when you define our human problem as having to do with bad examples, then our solution must provide a better example; when you define our human problem as narratively driven, then our solution must provide a better narrative to live and lean into.

REIMAGINING THE KINGDOM

Perhaps more significantly, our definition of the One who bore our solution, Jesus of Nazareth, is reduced to a prophet-like character who came simply to provide us a better example and better story to live; He came to change our environment in order to change us. So what's important about Jesus becomes His life and way of living. This means He doesn't have to be God and doesn't have to actually be alive.

If I have learned anything in the last few years, it's that theology matters, and when you get the pieces of theology wrong you ultimately get the gospel wrong. Of late, my generation is all a flutter with reimagining the Christian faith—reimagining the *pieces* of the Christian faith. I understand this pull toward reimagining the Christian faith, because I have been there myself. But what I have learned, especially at the end of my ThM and thesis project, is that what my generation needs is not to reimagine the Christian faith, but *rediscover* it. We need to rediscover what and how the Church of Jesus Christ has always believed about our problem, solution, and the One who bore that solution. We need to rediscover the gospel.

To be frank, that rediscovery effort is not going to come through the Emergent Church. It is clear their reimagination enterprise is simply one iteration in a long line of Protestant liberal leavers—Emergents have left the historic Christian faith in the same way liberals have every generation since Schleiermacher, yet in a way that's palatable for our postmodern, post-Christian day. Which, for this post-Emergent who had high hopes of a genuine third way that

Afterword

cuts through the malaise of contemporary liberal-conservative theologic discourse, is sad indeed.

As is probably evident at this point, this book and the thesis project that went into it is deeply personal. It's personal because I myself was involved with and hoodwinked by the Emergent Church. And it's personal because I myself still long for a third way. I realize this term is over used, yet as I survey our current evangelical landscape that is split between progressive Emergent evangelicals on the one side and traditional Young Calvinist evangelicals on the other, I'm left wanting. I—and my gut tells me plenty more people—want an alternative that cuts through the current evangelical malaise and recaptures the gospel in all of its grandeur and majesty and revolutionary character—a gospel that includes the Kingdom in all of its already-not-yet glory in order to provide new life right now.

Now more than ever the Church is in need of passionate ambassadors of Christ who take seriously their calling as ministers of reconciliation, in the fullest sense of that Kingdom calling. Yet, I hope that a new generation of Christians will rediscover what the Church has always believed regarding God's magical, revolutionary Story of Rescue in order to bring the type of right-now transformation for which our world longs—without reimagining the Kingdom, and consequently the gospel, along the way.

In closing this book, I would be remise if I didn't acknowledge the real "man behind the curtain" who made this work possible: my advisor, mentor, and friend Michael E. Wittmer, who graciously provided the foreword to this work. In many ways, Mike's patience, push-backs, and prodding launched my journey beyond Emergent. Several conversations over several Chinese lunches and even more conversations in my academic program challenged me to search the scriptures, hold on to tradition, and rediscover—rather than reimagine—what the Church has always believed.

So thanks, Mike. I would not have made it this far if it was not for you. And I will make it even further thanks to your care and friendship—and some more Chinese lunches.

BIBLIOGRAPHY

Barth, Karl. *Protestant Thought: From Rousseau to Ritschl.* New York: Harper and Brothers, 1959.

Belcher, Jim. *Deep Church: A Third Way Beyond Emerging and Traditional.* Downers Grove: IVP Books, 2009.

Clements, Keith W. *Friedrich Schleiermacher: Pioneer of Modern Theology.* London: Collins Liturgical Publications, 1987.

Cooper, John W. *Panentheism: The Other God of the Philosophers.* Grand Rapids: BakerAcademic, 2006.

Dorrien, Gary. "Kingdom Coming: Rauschenbusch's Christianity and the Social Crisis." *Christian Century* 124 no 24 (2007): 25-29.

Fries, Paul Roy. "Religion and the Hope for a Truly Human Existence." PhD diss., Utrecht University, 1979.

Garvie, Alfred Ernest. *The Ritschlian Theology, Critical and Constructive*. Edinburgh: T & T Clark, 1899.

Gibbs, Eddie and Ryan K. Bolger. *Emerging Churches: Creating Christian Community in Postmodern Cultures*. Grand Rapids: BakerAcademic, 2005.

Grenz, Stanley J. and Roger E. Olson. *20th Century Theology: God and the World in a Transitional Age*. Downers Grove: InterVarsity Press, 1992.

Grenz, Stanley J. *A Primer on Postmodernism*. Grand Rapids: Eerdmans Publishing, 1996.

Jones, Tony. *The New Christians: Dispatches from the Emergent Frontier*. San Francisco: Jossey-Bass, 2008.

Killen, R. Allan. The Ontological Theology of Paul Tillich. Kampen, J. H. Kok, 1956.

Livingston, James C. *Modern Christian Thought: From the Enlightenment to Vatican II*. New York: Macmillian, 1971.

McLaren, Brian. *The Story We Find Ourselves In*. San Francisco: Jossey-Bass, 2003.

_____. *A Generous Orthodoxy*. Grand Rapids: Zondervan, 2004.

Bibliography

———. *The Secret Message of Jesus*. Nashville: Word Publishing, 2006.

———. *Everything Must Change*. Nashville: Thomas Nelson Publishers, 2007.

———. "Church Emerging: Why I Still Use the Word Postmodern but with Mixed Feelings." Pages 141-152 in *An Emergent Manifesto of Hope*. Edited by Doug Pagitt and Tony Jones. Grand Rapids: BakerBooks, 2007.

———. *A New Kind of Christianity*. New York: HarperOne, 2010.

Mueller, David L. *An Introduction to the Theology of Albrecht Ritschl*. Philadelphia: The Westminster Press, 1969.

Nelson, Derek R. "Schleiermacher and Ritschl on Individual and Social Sin." *Journal of the History of Modern Theology*. 16 no 2 (2009): 131-154.

Niebuhr, Richard R. *Schleiermacher on Christ and Religion*. New York: Scribner's, 1964.

O'Neill, Andrew. *Tillich: A Guide for the Perplexed*. New York: T & T Clark, 2008.

Olson, Roger. *The Story of Christian Theology*. Downers Grove: IVP Academic, 1999.

Orr, James. *The Ritschlian Theology and the Evangelical Faith*. London: Houghton and Stoughton, 1897.

Pauk, Wilhem and Marion. *Paul Tillich: His Life and Thought*. New York: Harper and Row, Publishers, 1989.

Raschke, Carl. *The Next Reformation: Why Evangelicals Must Embrace Postmodernity*. Grand Rapids: Baker Academic, 2004.

Rauschenbusch, Walter. *Christianity and the Social Crisis*. New York: HarperOne, 2007.

_____. *A Theology for the Social Gospel*. Nashville: Abingdon Press, 1945.

_____. *The Righteousness of the Kingdom*. Nashville: Abingdon Press, 1968.

Ritschl, Albrecht. *Instruction In The Christian Religion*. London: Longmans, Green, and Co., 1901.

_____. *The Christian Doctrine of Justification and Reconciliation*. Edinburgh: T & T Clark, 1902.

Schleiermacher, Friedrich. *On Religion: Speeches to Its Cultured Despisers*. New York: Harper Torchbooks, 1958.

_____. *The Christian Faith*. Philadelphia, Fortress Press, 1928.

_____. *Schleiermacher's Soliloquies: An English Translation of the Monologen with a Critical Introduction and Appendix*. Translated by Horace Leland Friess. Chicago: The Open Court Publishing Company, 1926.

Bibliography

Smith, James K. A. *Who's Afraid of Postmodernism: Taking Derrida, Lyotard, and Foucault to Church*. Grand Rapids: BakerAcademic, 2006.

Stackhouse, Max L. Introduction to *The Righteousness of the Kingdom*, by Walter Rauschenbusch. Edited by Max L. Stackhouse; New York: Abingdon Press, 1968.

Swing, Albert Temple. *The Theology of Albrecht Ritschl*. London: Longmans, Green, and Co., 1901.

Tillich, Paul. *The Shaking of the Foundations*. New York: Charles Scribner's Sons, 1948.

_____. *Systematic Theology* 3 vols. Chicago: The University of Chicago Press, 1951.

_____. "Victory in Defeat: The Meaning of History in Light of Christian Prophetism." *Interpretation* 6 (1952): 17-26.

_____. *The Courage to Be*. New Haven: Yale University Press, 1952.

_____. *The New Being*. New York: Charles Scribner's Sons, 1955.

_____. *The Eternal Now*. New York: Charles Scribner's Sons, 1963.

_____. "The Right to Hope." *The Christian Century* 107 no 33 (1990): 1064-1067.

Welch, Claude. *Protestant Thought in the Nineteenth Century.* 2 vols. Eugene, OR: Wipf & Stock Publishers, 2003.

West, Cornell. "Can These Dry Bones Live?" Pages 231-234 in *Christianity and the Social Crisis in the 21st Century.* Edited by Paul Rauschenbusch; New York: HarperOne, 2007.

Wyman, Walter E. "Sin and Redemption." Pages 129-149 in *The Cambridge Companion to Friedrich Schleiermacher.* Edited by Jaqueline Mariña. Cambridge: Cambridge University Press, 2005.

www.ingramcontent.com/pod-product-compliance
Lightning Source LLC
Chambersburg PA
CBHW020931090426
42736CB00010B/1104